Aaron Max

Jake Kobre Smith

20 EVENTS

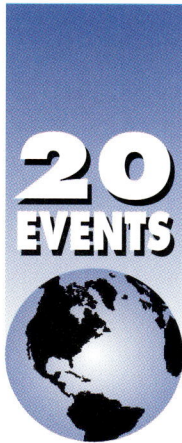

Transportation

MILESTONES AND BREAKTHROUGHS

RICHARD STEINS

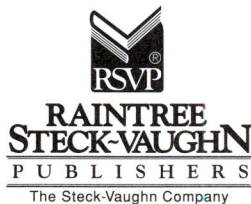

RSVP
RAINTREE
STECK-VAUGHN
PUBLISHERS
The Steck-Vaughn Company

Austin, Texas

Consultant: Gary Gerstle, Department of History, The Catholic University of America, Washington, D.C.

**Developed for Steck-Vaughn Company by
Visual Education Corporation, Princeton, New Jersey**

Project Director: Jewel Moulthrop
Editor: Michael Gee
Copy Editor: Margaret P. Roeske
Editorial Assistants: Carol Ciaston, Stacy Tibbetts
Photo Research: Martin A. Levick
Production Supervisor: Maureen Ryan Pancza
Proofreading Management: William A. Murray
Word Processing: Cynthia C. Feldner
Interior Design: Maxson Crandall, Lee Grabarczyk
Cover Design: Maxson Crandall
Page Layout: Maxson Crandall, Lisa Evans-Skopas,
                      Christine Osborne

Raintree Steck-Vaughn Publishers staff

Editor: Shirley Shalit
Project Manager: Joyce Spicer

Library of Congress Cataloging-in-Publication Data

Steins, Richard.
   Transportation milestones and breakthroughs / Richard Steins.
      p.   cm. — (20 Events)
   Includes bibliographical references and index.
   ISBN 0-8114-4935-1
   1. Transportation—Juvenile literature. [1. Transportation—History.] I. Title. II. Series.
TA1149.S76 1995
629.04—dc20   94–17549
                                                      CIP
                                                      AC

Cover: Despite obstacles along the track, early trains (background) attained speeds of nearly 50 miles per hour. Today's high-speed trains, such as France's TGV (inset), carry passengers at speeds of 150 miles per hour or more.

Credits and Acknowledgments

Cover photos: *Held-Up,* Newbold H. Trotter, © 1994 Smithsonian Institution, Washington, D.C. (background), French Tourist Office (inset)
Illustrations: Parrot Graphics, Precision Graphics
Maps: Parrot Graphics

4: Comstock; **5:** Courtesy of Goodyear; **7:** Superstock; **8:** Gerald S. Ratliff/West Virginia Division of Tourism; **9:** Superstock; **10:** The Bettmann Archive (left), Air and Space Museum/Smithsonian Institution (right); **11:** Ferne Saltzman (top), Air and Space Museum/Smithsonian Institution (bottom); **12:** The Bettmann Archive; **13:** Paolo Koch/Photo Researchers (top), Nevada Tourism Commission (bottom); **14:** Library of Congress (top), Library of Congress (bottom); **15:** Mississippi Tourist Office; **16:** Library of Congress (top), Museum of the City of New York (bottom); **17:** Albany Institute of Art; **18:** The Bettmann Archive; **19:** Mary Evans Picture Library/Photo Researchers (top), Lawrence Migdale/Photo Researchers (bottom); **20:** Library of Congress (top), Brown Brothers (bottom); **21:** Peabody Essex Museum, Salem, MA, Photo by Mark Sexton; **22:** The Bettmann Archive; **23:** The Bettmann Archive (top), Marriott Corporation (bottom); **24:** Hulton-Deutsch Collection; **25:** UPI/Bettmann; **26:** Brown Brothers (top); Library of Congress (bottom); **27:** Amtrak (left), Amtrak (right); **28:** The Bettmann Archive; **29:** Martin A. Levick; **30:** UPI/Bettmann; **31:** UPI/Bettmann (top), Blair Seitz/Photo Researchers (bottom); **32:** Sikorsky Aircraft; **33:** Sikorsky Aircraft (top), Sikorsky Aircraft (bottom); **34:** AP/Wide World Photos (top); AP/Worldwide Photos (bottom); **36:** Air and Space Museum/Smithsonian Institution (left), Novosti/Science Photo Library/Photo Researchers (right); **37:** NASA; **38:** French Tourist Office; **39:** German Information Center (top), Japan Railways Group (bottom); **40:** Air and Space Museum/Smithsonian Institution; **41:** British Airways; **42:** Library of Congress; **43:** Paul MacCready/AeroVironment, Inc. (top), Paul MacCready/AeroVironment (bottom)

Contents

The Wheel

The development
of the wheel during
the Bronze Age
made transportation
over land possible.

The Stone Age

It is almost impossible to imagine any kind of human life without the wheel. The development of the wheel was so important that no other invention—indeed much of what we today regard as transportation—would have been possible without it.

About two million years ago, when human beings first appeared, they used crude chopping tools made from pebbles. For this reason, the period from two million years ago to about 3000 B.C.—when people began to make tools of bronze—is known as the Stone Age.

In human history, the wheel was a relatively late development. Thus far, archaeologists and anthropologists have not discovered any evidence of the wheel during the Stone Age.

The earliest humans were hunters and gatherers. They lived in small, nomadic groups roaming from place to place in search of food and shelter. Large communities of people did not exist in the sense that we know them today. Tools found from this time were made mostly of stone.

During the latter part of the Stone Age (about 8,000 years ago), humans began to settle in villages, cultivate plants, and domesticate animals. Handcrafts, such as pottery making and weaving, started to develop. There were more tools and different kinds of tools; but they were still made mostly of stone.

The Bronze Age

The term Bronze Age is used to define a period in the development of technology. Bronze is an alloy, or mixture, of copper and tin. To create bronze, copper and tin are melted and mixed, then shaped and cooled in some type of cast. The first known use of bronze was in Mesopotamia about 3500 B.C.

The discovery of metal tools proves that these ancient people had considerable knowledge of mining, smelting (the melting down of metals), and the casting of metals. Since supplies of raw materials were often outside the local area, travel to other regions began to develop. It is likely that the wheel developed because of the need to transport materials and people over substantial land distances.

Uses of Early Wheels It is not known who invented the first wheel or how it came into being. Interestingly, the first wheels, which date from the Bronze Age, were made of stone, not metal. Unlike many of today's wheels, which have spokes, these first wheels did not. In fact, they looked more like disks made of stone. The first spoked wheels appeared around 2700 B.C. Spoked wheels were lighter than the solid stone wheels and, therefore, were easier to use. They were immediately adopted for military use, where the demand for lighter-wheeled, faster vehicles was great. The design of the spoked wheel remained essentially the same until the coming of railroads in the 19th century and the automobile in the 20th century. Solid metal wheels were developed for railroad cars. Tubed tires—and later tubeless tires—were developed for the automobile.

Bronze Age wheels probably had a number of uses. Most likely, they

The earliest known wheels were made of stone and wood. Archaeologists have dated this one at about 2500 B.C.

were used in the making of pottery. The potter's wheel is still used today to spin clay rapidly as it is being shaped. Archaeologists believe that this technique probably developed during the Bronze Age.

Another use for wheels at this time was in agriculture. People and domesticated animals, such as horses and oxen, probably dragged crude carts that were mounted on two wheels.

Wheels as Machines The next great use for the wheel—to make work easier—developed slowly over the centuries. One of the first uses of the wheel as a machine was for lifting water. In its most basic form, the ancient *noria*—a device that was used to collect water for irrigation—consisted of a large wheel with paddles around its rim. Buckets were attached to the rim, and the wheel was partially submerged in a stream. The current turned the wheel, filling the buckets with water. As the buckets reached the top of the wheel, they tilted and emptied into a trough.

With the invention of the gear—a wheel with teeth or notches—the wheel became a device that transmitted force. When two such wheels are used together, they can enhance and transmit motion. For example, when the teeth of two gears mesh, turning one gear will cause the other to rotate. If the gears are attached to a shaft, the shaft also will rotate. Thus motion or force can be transferred from one shaft to another simply by the turning of the meshed gears. This basic movement was the basis of all machinery, regardless of its power source—water for paddle wheels, air for windmills.

Today's wheels come in all sizes. Some, like the ones on this mining vehicle, are taller than the people who use them.

ANCIENT PADDLE WHEEL

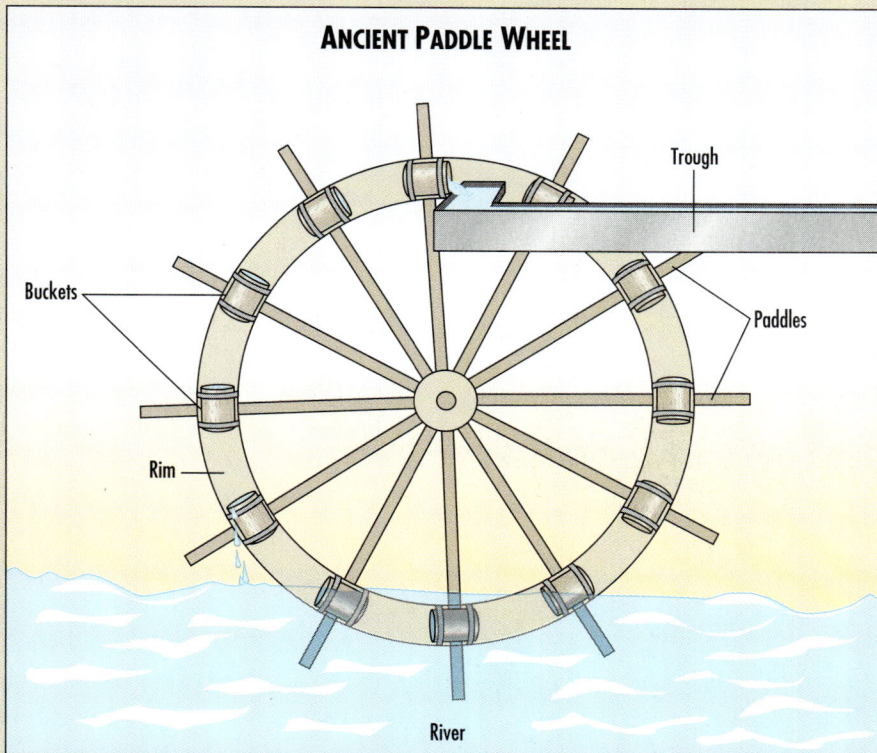

Trough

Buckets

Paddles

Rim

River

The river current moved the paddles on the rim of the wheel. Wooden buckets attached to the rim picked up water and deposited it in a trough that carried the water to the crops.

Without the Wheel, Unthinkable!

The wheel enabled all forms of transportation and many kinds of machines to develop. Wheels are so much a part of our lives today that their uses are too numerous to list. Just think of how many uses of wheels people encounter on a daily basis—trucks, buses, automobiles, tricycles, bicycles, push toys and pull toys, mechanical clocks and watches, elevators and escalators, assembly lines, cranes, pulleys, cement mixers, nuts and bolts . . . Where would we be today without the wheel? Many historians consider the wheel to be one of the greatest inventions in human history.

5

The Appian Way

This highway from Rome to the east was the most famous road of ancient times.

All Roads Lead to Rome

The Roman Empire flourished about 2,000 years ago. At the height of their power, the Romans occupied all of western Europe, northern Africa, Greece, and most of the Middle East. They even conquered parts of the British Isles.

As the empire expanded, the Romans realized the need to build a system of strong roads. These roads connected all parts of the empire and allowed Roman military forces to move quickly over long distances.

The great Roman roads were built over a period of centuries beginning about 400 years before the birth of Christ. Although designed for military use, they became equally important as avenues of trade and commerce. Romans traded their goods for products—such as spices—that came from the East.

Roman roads extended outward in all directions from the city of Rome. Today, the expression "all roads lead to Rome" derives from the time when Rome was the most important city and controlled the largest empire in the world.

In addition to facilitating transportation throughout the Roman Empire, the Appian Way came to symbolize the enormous power of the Roman leaders.

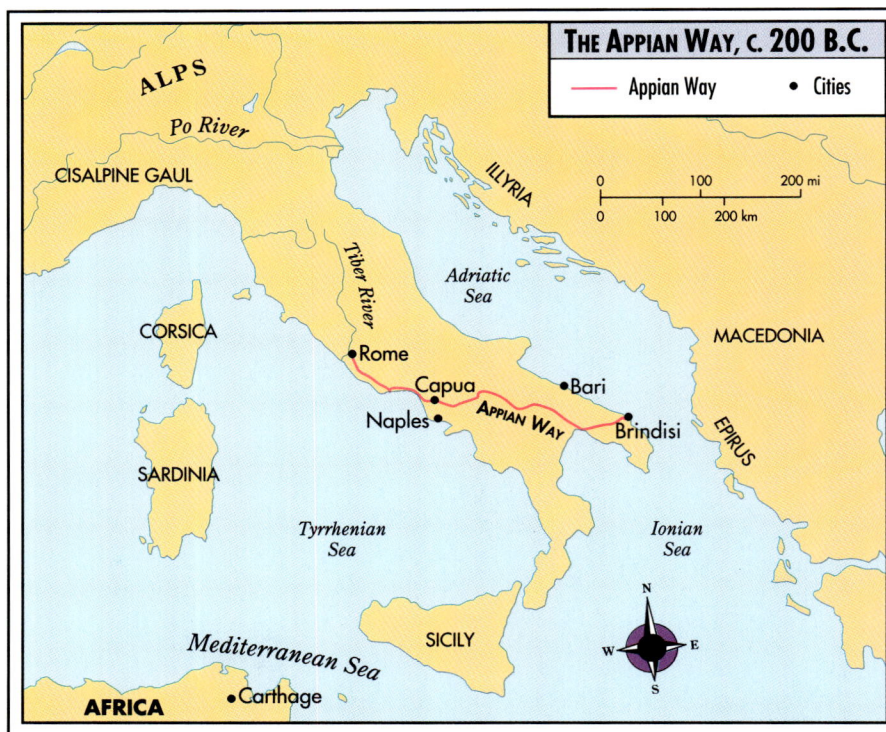

THE APPIAN WAY, c. 200 B.C.
— Appian Way • Cities

A New Kind of Road

The most famous Roman road was the Appian Way. Its construction began in 312 B.C. under censor Appius Claudius Caecus, for whom it was named. The first section of the road extended 132 miles southeast to the town of Capua. A branch was built later to the Adriatic port city of Brindisi, about 235 miles away. Other sections built over the years connected Rome with Naples, Bari, and other port cities.

In comparison to today's superhighways, the Appian Way was extremely small in length and width. But 2,000 years ago, it was gigantic.

Strong Construction Because the Appian Way was meant to carry troops and heavy equipment, it had to be strong and well constructed. Unlike other roads of the time—which were mainly simple dirt paths—the Appian Way had several layers of stone and cement. At the base were stone blocks cemented together with a lime mortar. The surface of the road—about 20 feet wide—may have originally been covered with gravel. Later, however, it was covered with layered blocks of lava. The Appian Way was higher in the middle than at the sides, a design that allowed water to drain off.

Because of its well-planned construction with layered stone, the Appian Way endured the heavy traffic to which it was subjected over the centuries—military forces, travelers, and traders with their goods. Throughout its history, the Appian Way was regularly maintained and repaired. A high-ranking official was assigned the sole job of making sure that the Appian Way did not fall into disrepair. The Romans realized that it was a major link in their network of roads extending to the outer reaches of the empire.

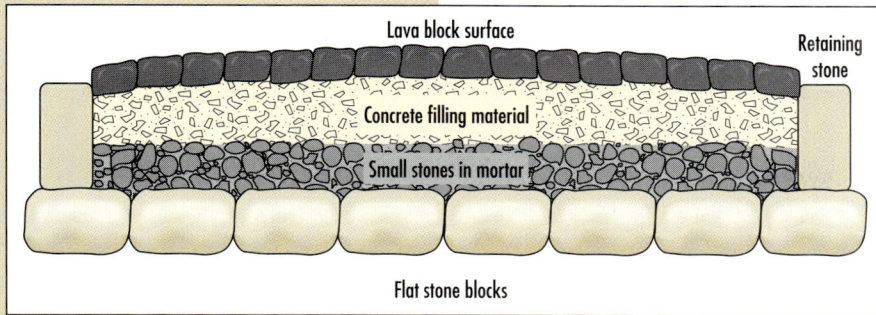

Lava block surface
Retaining stone
Concrete filling material
Small stones in mortar
Flat stone blocks

The remarkably engineered Roman roads curved downward toward the sides to allow excess rainwater to flow into ditches.

A Focal Point Because so many thousands of people traveled along the road, the Appian Way became a kind of focal point. Tombs and monuments were built along the road, and some of their ruins are visible today. Early Christians sought refuge from persecution in the catacombs (underground passageways) along the Appian Way. One of the surviving structures from the early Christian era is the Church of St. Sebastian, near Rome, and its catacombs.

Government leaders also used the Appian Way for a gruesome display of their power. Public executions by crucifixion were a familiar sight on the road to visitors as they approached Rome. Travelers to and from Rome were thereby easily reminded of the power of the empire and the punishment that awaited those who broke its laws.

Uniting the Empire The great network of roads allowed Romans—both military and civilian—to move quickly to the outer reaches of their empire. But these roads also allowed non-Romans to travel to Rome. By these roads, Roman culture was spread throughout Europe, northern Africa, and the Middle East, and non-Roman culture was brought to the empire.

The Legacy of Roman Roads

Historic roads are among the many legacies left to Western civilization by the Romans. In addition to the Appian Way, the Romans built roads to the north and throughout other parts of western Europe and the British Isles. In London today, Watling Street—which goes from that city northwest to the town of Saint Albans—was originally a Roman road. Even after the collapse of the empire around A.D. 400, Roman roads remained an important means of transportation for all Europeans.

Modern highways have come a long way from the construction of the Appian Way. Today, major roads no longer are made of brick and cement but are paved with asphalt. Unlike the Roman roads, which were all designed to run in a straight line, modern roads have curves and travel through rugged terrain.

But many Roman engineering principles are still in evidence in modern road construction. For example, the principle of layered roadbeds and a design that allows for drainage are both innovations that were pioneered by the Romans.

Many of the ancient Roman roads have been replaced by modern highways. This section in Italy has remained much as it was in ancient times.

The Conestoga Wagon

By enabling people to transport heavy loads over long distances, this unusual vehicle helped open the West to settlement.

Before the development of the Conestoga wagon, early settlers were limited by the great natural boundary of the Allegheny Mountains and the nearby dense forests.

Travel in Early America

Throughout much of U.S. history, Americans have yearned to move westward. But in the 1700s, travel from the East to the West was extremely difficult. Inland from the eastern seaboard lay a great obstacle—the Allegheny Mountains. The lack of good roads through the mountains left travelers with few choices. They could travel in a roundabout way by river, but most rivers in the East run in a north-south direction. Or they could struggle with horse and wagon through the dense forests and over the Alleghenies toward the West.

A familiar sight in colonial America was the horse train, also called the packtrain. This was a caravan of horses and travelers who banded together for long trips westward.

The tedious journey across the Alleghenies was frustrating for both the farmers of the West and the merchants and shippers of the East. The farmers needed to get their goods to eastern markets. Merchants in the East had fabric, clothing, and tools that farmers desperately needed.

A Long-distance Wagon

Early wagons were inadequate for long journeys over rough terrain. They were small, flat-bottomed, and able to carry only limited loads.

It was far easier for the traveler simply to travel on horseback through the dense, unsettled forests. But very little—in fact, close to nothing—could be transported by a single horse aside from the rider. And even horse trains could carry only so much. Americans solved the problem of transporting heavy loads by developing a stronger and larger wagon for the long and difficult east-west journey. This innovation was called the Conestoga wagon, named after the Conestoga region of Pennsylvania, where the wagon was developed.

Conestoga wagons first came into use around 1725. For the next 100 years, they carried most of the goods and people that crossed the Alleghenies to the Ohio Valley.

A Sturdy Design Instead of the usual flat bottom, the Conestoga wagon's was curved. This curved shape formed a well and prevented the wagon's contents from shifting as it traveled through mountain passes and lurched along uneven ground. The front and the back of the wagon were higher than the middle, thereby enhancing the well-like function. The Conestoga's wheels were much wider than the wheels on ordinary wagons. This design feature prevented the wagon from sinking in the mud during rainy weather.

To protect the wagon's occupants and goods from bad weather, a rounded canvas hood with arched openings at the front and rear covered the wagon. Amazingly, Conestoga wagons could also float and serve as temporary boats to cross streams and rivers. Because it was a

The Conestoga wagon was specially constructed to carry large amounts of goods, to withstand the rigors of early cross-country travel, and to protect travelers from bad weather. The early pioneers usually traveled in wagon trains for their mutual protection and company on the long journey.

heavy wagon—especially when full—the Conestoga needed to be pulled by a team of six to eight horses.

Wagon Trains to the West Conestoga wagon trains soon replaced horse trains as the principal means of traveling over the Allegheny Mountains. On the journey from the eastern seaboard, the Conestogas carried fabric, clothing, farm tools, machinery, and food products not grown in the Midwest.

And, of course, they carried new settlers, their families, and all the household goods people could take with them on the long trip westward. Because of the Conestogas, more people in the 1700s were able to cross the Alleghenies and settle on the wide-open western plains.

On the return trip from the West to the East, the wagon trains would be laden with farm products, such as wheat, corn, and other grains. These farm products were sold in cities, such as New York, Boston, Albany, and Philadelphia. What was not sold in the East was shipped overseas for sale in Europe.

For more than a century, Conestoga wagons served as the link between the commercial centers of the East and the western frontier. The wagons—which some people called "camels of the prairie"—came to symbolize early American travel and the courageous pioneering spirit of the American people.

▶ This excerpt is from the diary of Catherine Haun, who, as a young bride, crossed the plains by wagon train in the 1800s.

The End of an Era

The prominence of the Conestoga wagon in long-distance travel was gradually challenged by two other transportation innovations. The first was the building of canals in the Northeastern United States in the 1820s and 1830s. Canal building made east-west travel even faster and cheaper. Using the Erie Canal in upstate New York, for example, farmers could ship their products by barge to markets in the East even more quickly than by wagon train.

But the most important innovation was the development of railroads. The era of significant railroad building in the United States began in the 1850s. Thousands of miles of track were laid over the next 50 years. Gradually, a network of railroads linked all parts of the country, making travel relatively safe, quick, and inexpensive.

A variation of the Conestoga wagon—called a prairie schooner—came into use when settlers moved across the Great Plains in the late 1800s. Long-distance travel however, was increasingly done by railroad.

One family . . . man, wife and two little girls . . . had only a large . . . wagon drawn by four mules and a meager but well chosen supply of food and feed. A tent was strapped to one side of the wagon, a roll of bedding to the other . . . baggage, bundles, pots, pans and bags of horse feed hung on behind . . . [the man] being an expert driver . . . required but little help thus being a desirable member of the train.

Montgolfier Brothers' Balloon

In 1783, Joseph and Jacques Montgolfier invented the first practical balloon.

Joseph Montgolfier (left) never completed his education, having run away from home as a teenager. However, he was an avid reader of scientific material. Jacques Montgolfier's training as an architect provided him with a strong background in science and technology.

Fascinated by Flight

Humans have always had a fascination with flying. Greek mythology includes the story of Icarus, who attempted to fly with wings made of wax and feathers. According to the myth, Icarus flew too close to the sun. The wings melted, and he fell to his death.

Humans also were fascinated with making devices and machines that could fly. One of the early interests in flight involved balloons. But what would make a balloon rise above the earth and fly?

In 1766, British scientist Henry Cavendish discovered that the substance hydrogen was seven times lighter than air. If a lighter-than-air gas could fill a balloon, then the balloon might rise. Another idea involved air itself and the principle of hot air rising. Air could be used to fill a balloon. Increasing a flame in the basket below the balloon would heat the air in the balloon, making it rise. Lowering the flame would lower the balloon. Once inventors understood that balloons would rise by lighter-than-air gases or by hot air itself, ballooning was ready to take off.

Early Balloon Flights

In 1783, two French brothers, Joseph Michel and Jacques Étienne Montgolfier, invented the first practical balloon. The brothers believed that smoke from the flame made a balloon rise. But they soon discovered that hot air, and not the smoke, propelled the balloon upward.

Montgolfier Balloons The Montgolfier brothers' first successful balloon flight occurred near Lyons, France, on June 5, 1783. Their balloon, which was made of linen cloth and paper, was about 35 feet in diameter. It rose on a cloud of hot air and smoke, stayed aloft for ten minutes, and traveled about one mile.

On this first balloon trip, no human or animal was on board. Three months later, however, the brothers sent up another balloon. This time, the balloon carried a duck, a rooster, and a sheep. When the animals returned unharmed after an eight-minute flight, the Montgolfiers were ready to launch a human being.

The first manned flight occurred on October 15, 1783. On that day, French scientist François Pilâtre de Rozier rose 80 feet into the air on board a Montgolfier balloon that remained tied to the ground. In

▶ Reports of the flight included this eyewitness account by a nearby landowner: *The Montgolfiers have just performed a really curious spectacle here, that of a machine made of cloth and covered with paper which had the shape of a house. . . . They made it ascend by means of a fire to a prodigious height. . . . My peasants who saw it, . . . believed it was the moon falling from the sky . . . .*

November of the same year, Pilâtre de Rozier and a companion rose 300 feet in the air above Paris.

Other Experiments Soon other inventors began their own experiments with balloons. In 1783, French chemist Jacques Alexandre Charles traveled 15 miles in a hydrogen-filled balloon. In 1785, an American doctor named John Jeffries and a French balloonist, Jean-Pierre Blanchard, made the first balloon flight across the English Channel. The trip, from Dover, England, to Calais, France, took two hours.

The early pioneers of balloon flight were mainly interested in rising off the ground. But soon others began to look for practical uses for balloons. The early balloon makers and fliers probably had little idea of the variety of ways this vehicle would be put to use in later centuries.

Balloon flight is still important—both for pleasure and for scientific research.

Practical Uses for Balloons

Wartime Uses One of the most important practical uses for balloons was in war. In the American Civil War in the 1860s, for example, the military used balloons tethered to the ground to observe enemy troop movements. During World War II in the 1940s, balloons tethered to the ground were used as obstacles and protection against low-flying fighter aircraft. Called barrage balloons, they floated perhaps 100 feet above the earth, thereby preventing enemy aircraft from flying too close to the ground. Barrage balloons were a familiar sight over London during the German raids on that city.

Dirigibles and Blimps Another practical variation on the balloon was the dirigible. A dirigible (also called an airship) is a giant cigar-shaped balloon with a fixed metal interior frame, attached to a passenger cabin and engines. In the early 20th century, dirigibles were considered as a possible means of passenger travel. But they proved dangerous and impractical. Several airships were wrecked in storms. Then, with the explosion of the hydrogen-filled German dirigible *Hindenburg* in 1937 over Lakehurst, New Jersey, the age of dirigible travel ended.

Blimps, however, have continued to thrive. Although a blimp looks similar to a dirigible, it has no fixed metal frame and rises and falls using helium. Most modern blimps are used for sightseeing or advertising.

Science and Recreation Balloons are used today both for scientific research and for pleasure. Meteorologists and astronomers often use high-flying balloons—manned or unmanned, and carrying sophisticated electronic equipment—to examine the properties of cosmic rays and to study weather patterns.

Pleasure balloons, however, seem to have unending variety and use—from the toy balloons children play with to hot-air-balloon pleasure flights and races.

11

Invented over
two centuries ago,
the bicycle still
is used today
for transportation
and recreation.

This early bicycle was constructed in 1817 by Baron Karl von Drais. Propelled by the rider's feet, this vehicle had a steering bar that enabled the rider to change direction.

Bi = Two; Cycle = Wheel

No one is quite certain why, but two-wheeled devices propelled by human feet first appeared in France in the 1790s. Comte Mede de Sivrac invented a wooden vehicle that resembled a scooter. He called it a *célérifère*. This contraption had no pedals or steering mechanism. The rider stood on top of the frame and pushed with his or her feet. This device enabled people to move more quickly over short distances.

In 1816, German inventor Baron Karl von Drais added a steering bar to a two-wheeled vehicle. This bar was connected to the front wheel. It could be used to change the direction in which the vehicle was traveling. Drais's bicycle came to be known as a *draisine*. Although the draisine could be steered, it had one main drawback, which was that riders still had to move it forward by pushing against the ground with their feet.

A Fine Dandy Horse

Draisines were introduced in England around 1818. The bicycles we are all familiar with today evolved slowly during the early 1800s, as other European inventors sought ways to improve the basic design of the draisine. In 1839, a Scottish blacksmith named Kirkpatrick MacMillan had the idea of adding foot pedals.

MacMillan's pedals were actually a complicated mechanism consisting of rods and cranks. But the first step toward making a bicycle easier to drive had been taken. These early bicycles soon became known as "dandy horses," probably because riders looked a bit silly riding on a vaguely horse-shaped metal frame.

Around 1865, French inventor and carriage maker Pierre Lallement built a bicycle whose wooden wheels were covered with iron treads. He also made the front wheel larger than the rear wheel. The larger front wheel became a widely adopted innovation in the 1800s. Unfortunately, the pedals were attached to the front

wheel. Since this put them a great distance from the seat, Lallement's bicycle was virtually unusable by short people.

Partly in response to the needs of short men, women, and children, the tricycle—a three-wheeled device with two wheels at the rear—was invented. It became popular during the 1880s.

Safety Innovations Bicycles with large front wheels required long legs and considerable strength to operate. They also were difficult to steer. A fall from one of these early vehicles was unpleasant, and sometimes dangerous.

By the 1880s, bicycle design was moving in two directions. The first was intended to make it easier to pedal. The second was to improve its safety. For greater ease of pedaling, front wheels were made smaller. Eventually, both front and rear wheels were the same size.

To improve safety, the pedal mechanisms were attached to the rear wheel. This improvement gave the rider greater control over steering. In 1879, a British inventor named Harry J. Lawson produced the first bicycle that connected the pedals to the rear wheel by means of a sprocket-chain drive.

In 1888, the air-filled rubber tire was invented. When used on bicycles, these tires reduced the weight of the vehicle and made it safer. Other improvements included the hollow-steel frame, hand brakes, adjustable handlebars, and gears that made the bicycle easier to use. From a clumsy, foot-driven scooter, the bicycle had evolved to become a device that most people could use.

The Bicycle Craze Bicycling became an enormous fad in Europe and the United States during the 1880s. It was one of the few physical activities that men and women could share. Entire families took bicycle outings in the country. Bicycle clubs formed in the United States. One such organization, the League of American Wheelmen, urged the government to improve the conditions of roads. The growing popularity of the automobile in the early 20th century ended the bicycle fad—but only temporarily.

In China and many other countries around the world, bicycling is a major means of transportation.

A Fad Becomes a Way of Life

By the mid-20th century, bicycling also had become a recognized sport. One of the earliest official bicycle races was the famous Tour de France, established in 1903. The Tour de France is an annual event in which the world's best bicyclists compete in a marathon race more than 2,500 miles long. Bicycling is now a recognized Olympic sport.

During the 1970s, bicycling once again became a popular sport in the United States. Many people realized the healthful benefits that bicycling exercise provided. In addition, bicycles were relatively inexpensive, pollution-free, and easy to store. Practically everyone could ride a bicycle if he or she chose to do so.

But above all, bicycling is a major means of transportation throughout the world. Despite the automobile, bicycles are still widely used in Europe as a means of getting from one place to another. In other countries, such as China, the bicycle is the primary means of transportation for most of the population. Millions of Chinese citizens of all ages use their bicycles to go to work, to shop, or just to visit other people in the community. For the Chinese, bicycling is not merely a sport, but a vital part of their daily lives.

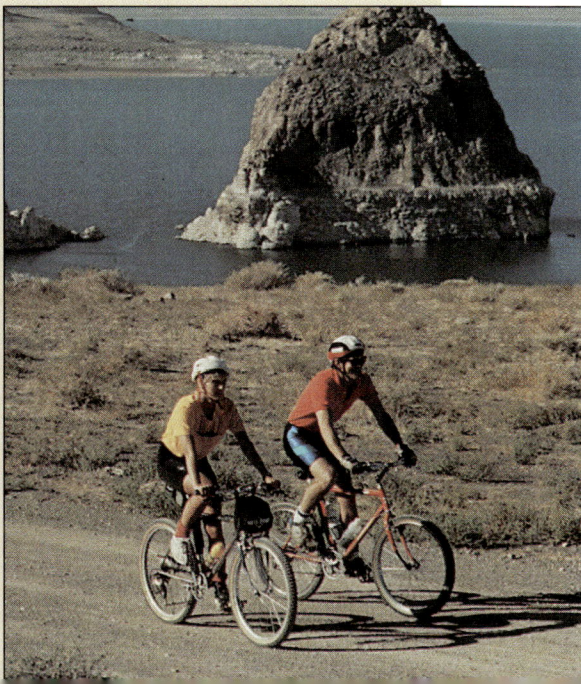

Ever since their invention, bicycles have been extremely popular. Today's bicycle manufacturers offer a wide variety—lightweight cycles for racing, sturdy ones for children, and rugged mountain bikes, such as the ones shown here.

13

The Clermont

With the launch of the *Clermont*, Robert Fulton proved that steamships could be commercially successful.

Robert Fulton, engineer and painter, was hired by Robert Livingston to design a steamboat that could carry passengers as well as cargo.

Steam Power and Boats

In 1712, when Thomas Newcomen harnessed steam to create power, he presented a variety of new opportunities for inventors. Shipbuilders were fascinated by the prospect of using a steam engine to drive boats, which for centuries had relied on wind and sail or on oars to move.

In the 1780s, an American inventor named James Rumsey used a steam engine to power a small boat along the Potomac River near Washington, D.C. David Fitch, another American inventor, built a steam-powered boat in 1790 that moved along the Delaware River. However, he never attracted enough passengers, and his project failed.

These early steamboats were designed to travel on rivers and in bays and other sheltered inland waterways. Sail-powered boats faced great difficulties in rivers, where swift currents and winds could shift suddenly. Bays were subject to rising and falling tides, which made sail navigation difficult. A steamboat, however, had enough steady power and forward thrust to overcome currents and tidal changes. And, of course, it was not dependent solely on the wind.

On its maiden voyage, Fulton himself piloted the *Clermont*.

Livingston and Fulton

Robert Livingston, a wealthy New York businessman, owned a monopoly on steamboat navigation on the Hudson River. He was interested in developing a new kind of vessel that could earn him more money. In 1802, Livingston hired inventor Robert Fulton to design and build a steamboat that would carry passengers and cargo on the Hudson River in New York State.

Born in Lancaster County, Pennsylvania, in 1765, Robert Fulton was an engineer and a painter as well as an inventor. He had been a gunsmith during the American Revolution, but he soon turned to portrait painting. Fulton always had an interest in mechanical devices. Over the years, he had created a number of inventions, including an underwater torpedo. When Fulton accepted Livingston's offer, he set about to design and build what at the time would be the largest steamboat ever launched.

A Triumph Robert Fulton's new steamboat, called the *Clermont*, was more than 140 feet long and 13 feet wide. It had a depth of 9 feet below the waterline.

The *Clermont* had a 20-foot copper boiler that generated steam from water heated by wood and coal. The steam that came out of the boiler went into a cylinder that contained a piston. This piston was attached to two paddle wheels, one on each side of the boat. Each paddle wheel was 15 feet in diameter and had eight 4-foot-wide paddles. As the paddle wheels turned, they moved the ship forward. The speed was a steady 5 miles per hour.

A Journey up the Hudson The design and construction of the *Clermont* took five years. By 1807, the vessel was ready to make its first voyage. For this first trip—from New York City to the state capital at Albany—Robert Fulton himself piloted the ship. The 150-mile journey was completed in 32 hours—a record time. (A sail-powered boat took at least four days to make the same trip.) The return trip took only 30 hours. Traveling on board the *Clermont* was far more comfortable than on any previous craft. Although much noisier than sail-driven vessels, the steam-powered boat's steady pace on the water made for a less rocky voyage. The *Clermont* was also equipped below deck with sleeping compartments and with other comforts previously unheard of on riverboats. On its open upper deck, passengers could stroll about. Or they could seek protection from the weather while sitting beneath a canopy at the rear of the vessel.

The *Clermont* was an instant success. Soon other steamboats were making regular trips on the Potomac, the Delaware, and even the Mississippi and Ohio rivers.

The Steamboat Revolution

The *Clermont* ushered in a revolutionary new age in ship travel. It proved that steam-driven vessels were profitable, comfortable, and fast. This, in turn, dramatically improved the transport of goods on major inland rivers, such as the Ohio and the Mississippi, making river cities like Cincinnati and St. Louis booming centers of manufacturing and trade.

Steamboat travel became popular a few years before the era of canal building in the United States. More than 3,000 miles of canals were built during the 1820s and 1830s to transport goods to and from the Midwest. Although steamboats were banned from the canals for fear of damage to the earthen banks, river journeys continued as an important way for early Americans and goods to travel.

Perhaps one of the most enduring symbols of 19th-century America is the Mississippi paddle wheeler, a steamboat directly descended from Fulton's *Clermont*. Like their predecessor, most Mississippi River steamboats had a paddle wheel on each side. A few had a single paddle at the rear of the boat. In the mid-1800s, Mississippi steamboats carried cotton and tobacco to the port of New Orleans, on the Gulf of Mexico, and transported passengers all along that mighty river. Mississippi paddle wheelers still can be seen today, although most are pleasure boats that specialize in river tours.

Ultimately, the most revolutionary effects of steam travel occurred in international travel and trade. By the late 19th century, steamships had cut travel time between the United States and England from several months to a few weeks. These oceangoing steamships used propellers rather than paddle wheels, but their engines were built on the same principles that Fulton had used on the *Clermont*.

Paddle wheel steamboats became an important mode of transportation on the Mississippi River. Steamboats, such as the *Mississippi Queen* and the *Delta Queen,* are immensely popular with tourists.

The Erie Canal

The Erie Canal eased travel between the Northeast and the Midwest and led to a wave of canal building in the United States.

A Route to the Midwest

In the early 1800s, the population of the United States was expanding inland beyond the eastern seaboard and the original 13 colonies. Settlers were moving in increasing numbers to the Midwest—to what is now Ohio, Indiana, and Illinois—and beyond.

But travel in the early 1800s was difficult and time-consuming. Conestoga wagon trains enabled merchants and farmers to ship heavy loads, but the trip still took a long time. A journey by horse-drawn wagon between New York City and Buffalo, New York, took as long as three weeks. (The same trip today takes about an hour by airplane.) During such a long journey, the traveler endured unpaved, bumpy roads and the dangers found in dense forests.

Americans needed a new way to connect the two parts of the country. Farmers in the Midwest wanted to transport their products to the east coast as quickly and as cheaply as possible.

Digging "Clinton's Ditch"

Some business and government leaders thought of a way to meet these needs. They proposed digging a canal across New York State, connecting Albany (on the Hudson River) with Buffalo (on Lake Erie). Such a canal would open the entire Great Lakes region to the east coast.

The leading supporter of the idea was the governor of New York, DeWitt Clinton. He was so closely associated with the proposed project that opponents ridiculed the idea by calling it "Clinton's ditch."

Difficult Conditions With a combination of financing from the state and private businesses, construction on the Erie Canal began in 1817. The engineers who built the canal were largely self-taught, for there were no engineering schools in the United States in the early 1800s.

The thousands of laborers who cleared the land and dug the canal over the next eight years—many of whom were Irish immigrants—worked under harsh conditions. The terrain was not mountainous, but there were many hills and forested

From the beginning, DeWitt Clinton—then governor of New York—was a strong supporter of the canal.

areas that needed clearing. The engineers devised elaborate systems of gears and pulleys to remove trees before the canal itself could be dug. In addition, unsanitary living conditions caused illness among the workers, and many died.

Despite these obstacles, the Erie Canal was completed in 1825. It was 363 miles long, 40 feet wide, and about 4 feet deep. Workers had constructed pathways on both sides of the canal for horses and mules to tow

The opening of the Erie Canal was celebrated by dignitaries and ordinary citizens. One artist covered the event with this drawing.

The Erie Canal had 83 locks, such as this one near Albany, to compensate for the difference in water levels between the Hudson River and Lake Erie.

the barges. Stone aqueducts carried the canal over streams. Workers constructed 83 stone and brick locks with heavy wooden gates along the length of the canal. This system of locks enabled barges to overcome the elevation difference between the Hudson River (at sea level) and Lake Erie (571 feet above sea level).

To celebrate the completion of the Erie Canal, Governor Clinton sailed on the barge, the *Seneca Chief,* from Buffalo to New York City. There, in a ceremony attended by many dignitaries, he emptied a barrel of Lake Erie water into the Hudson River. The Midwest and the east coast were now joined by water.

An Instant Success The new Erie Canal was an immediate success. The tolls that canal travelers had to pay brought a windfall of money to New York State. By opening a more direct connection between the Northeast and the Midwest, travel time and shipping costs were substantially reduced. For example, before the canal, four horses needed a full day to pull one ton of goods a mere two miles. On the Erie Canal, however, only two horses could pull a 100-ton barge a full 24 miles in a single day.

With speed came reduced shipping costs and lower prices for farm products. A new wave of prosperity came to New York City and to the towns and villages along the canal. The Erie Canal also led to an increase in westward migration and to a greater sense of unity between different sections of the country.

The vessel enters the lock, and the gates are closed behind it. The water level is raised or lowered to the level in the next section of the canal. The front gates open, and the vessel moves on.

The Legacy of the Erie Canal

The Erie Canal was a milestone in American transportation. In addition to the immediate prosperity it brought to farmers, businesspeople, and the government, it led to an explosion of canal building in the Northeast and the Midwest. By 1840, more than 3,300 miles of canals had been built in the United States, more than 20 times the mileage that existed in 1817. By the 1850s, canal building had begun to decline as railroads became a faster and cheaper means of travel.

However, the Erie Canal showed that government and business could work together on projects that benefited society. Today, for example, highway building often is financed by money from the federal and state governments and from the investment of private citizens and businesses.

Some parts of the original Erie Canal still exist today. They are part of a larger waterway called the New York State Barge Canal System. No longer used for commercial purposes, the canal is now home to numerous pleasure boats.

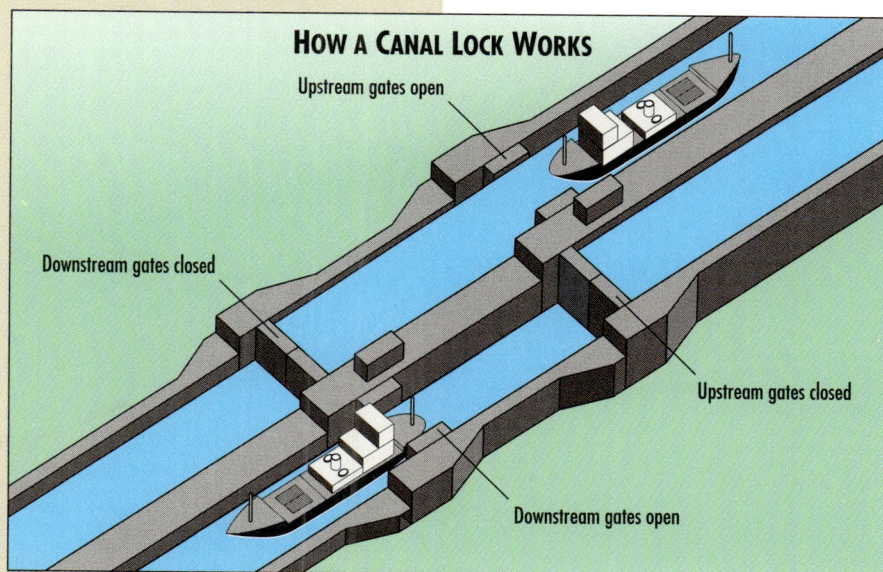

HOW A CANAL LOCK WORKS

Upstream gates open

Downstream gates closed

Upstream gates closed

Downstream gates open

The *Great Western*

One of the first
iron steamships,
the *Great Western* carried
passengers across
the Atlantic Ocean
in record time.

Transatlantic Travel

From the year 1620—when the Pilgrims arrived in New England on the *Mayflower*—until the early 1800s, very little changed in transatlantic travel. Ships were made of wood and powered by wind and sail. They were small and easily tossed about by storms. A trip from England to the New World could take anywhere from two to three months, depending on weather conditions. Every traveler knew the importance of luck in surviving the uncertainties and surprises of Atlantic Ocean weather.

By the early 1800s, Great Britain was the world's greatest seafaring power. But the wood Britain used to build its great navy and merchant fleet was growing scarce. To overcome this shortage of wood, British shipbuilders began to consider iron. Iron had many advantages over wood, especially for ships' hulls. Iron was far stronger than wood, and it did not rot as quickly from the effects of water. Furthermore, it was easier to repair.

The switch to iron marked the beginning of a new era in shipbuilding in Britain. With the addition of steam engines to power the new iron ships, a new age in sea travel began.

Steam and Iron

Steamships had crossed the Atlantic since the early 1800s. In 1819, an American ship—the *Savannah,* a small 90-foot vessel made of wood and powered by a steam engine—crossed from Savannah, Georgia, to Liverpool, England, in just 29 days. But the *Savannah* failed economically. Passengers were afraid to travel in a wooden ship that had a "fire in its belly."

After British shipbuilders began building iron ships, the situation changed. One of the first British iron ships was called the *Great Western.* Designed by the great naval architect Isambard Kingdom Brunel, the *Great Western* was launched in 1838. It was the first steamship designed specifically for regular transatlantic crossings—a business that the British were determined to develop.

A Strange Little Ship By today's standards, the *Great Western* was small and did not look like an ocean-going vessel. Only 236 feet long and 35 feet wide, it was scarcely 90 feet longer than Robert Fulton's river steamboat, the *Clermont.* In comparison to today's mighty ocean liners—such as the 1,000-foot-long *Queen Elizabeth II*—the *Great Western* seems impossibly small for a ship designed to cross the Atlantic Ocean.

The *Great Western* appeared to be a strange combination of different nautical design styles. Like the *Clermont,* it had two side paddle wheels that were driven by the ship's steam engines. The engines drove the ship

Isambard Kingdom Brunel, naval architect and railroad designer, built the first iron steamship specifically designed to carry passengers across the Atlantic Ocean.

Despite its small size, the *Great Western* began an age of transoceanic travel.

The First Ocean Liners

The *Great Eastern* was launched in 1858. It was 692 feet long and carried approximately 4,000 passengers in very cramped quarters. The *Great Eastern* also had side paddle wheels and the same combination of sail and steam. But the *Great Eastern* was a commercial failure. It was too large and could never fill up with enough paying passengers.

The age of iron ships that began with the *Great Western* lasted until the late 1800s, when shipbuilders began to switch to steel. It was lighter, stronger, and more flexible than iron. With less weight in their construction, ships could pick up more power and cross the Atlantic even faster. Continued improvements eventually produced the ocean liners of the 20th century that made the crossing in less than five days.

The *Great Western* and its successors represented a new age in transatlantic travel. As crossing the Atlantic became safer and faster, the connection between the United States and Europe was strengthened, and more and more immigrants left their homelands in Europe to settle in America.

at about 9 miles an hour, compared to the 5 miles an hour that the *Clermont* traveled.

But the *Great Western* also had a full complement of sails, like any sailing ship. There was a good reason. If weather conditions were right, sails could harness the wind's power for additional speed. Also, if an engine broke down—a frequent occurrence in the early days of steam power—the ship could continue on its journey using only its sails.

A Trip Across the Sea However strange it may have looked, the *Great Western* was a vast improvement for the traveler over what had gone before. Its iron hull and steam-driven power alone gave the cautious traveler a greater sense of security.

Because of its power, the *Great Western* reduced the time it took to cross the Atlantic—from two or three months to about 15 days. People liked the relative speed of the trip.

Although many travelers today prefer the speed of an airplane, many others enjoy the luxury of a slower ocean cruise.

Clipper Ships

The famous slender ships designed for speedy delivery of cargo "clipped" time and distance off the trip.

In 1926, Donald McKay came to New York to work as an apprentice to master shipbuilder Isaac Webb. After more than 20 years in the industry, McKay established his own shipyard.

A Fast and Slender Ship

Clipper ships were slender sailing ships that were designed for speedy transport of cargo. They flourished during the mid-19th century and were used in trade between the United States, China, and Australia as well as in trade across the Atlantic Ocean.

Small, clipper-type ships had been built in the Chesapeake Bay area in the late 1700s and early 1800s. Known as Baltimore clippers, some were used to transport slaves before the slave trade was outlawed in 1808.

The name *clipper* arose because of the fast way in which these ships "clipped off" the miles. The early clippers sailed mostly in interior waters like the Chesapeake. But by the 1840s, a need arose for fast transoceanic cargo ships. The tea trade between China and the United States was growing, and merchants needed to get their goods quickly across the Pacific. In addition, the discovery of gold in California in 1848 led to a thriving commerce between the east and west coasts of the United States. The trip between coasts forced boats to circumnavigate South America, a distance of thousands of miles.

The Age of Clippers

The clipper ships designed to travel the ocean had two design features to guarantee maximum speed.

- The number of sails. The new clippers were square rigged and had three or more masts to accommodate an increased number of sails compared with earlier sailing vessels. Some of the new ships had as many as 35 sails.
- A slender hull. This enabled the ship to knife through the water at rapid speeds. Clippers generally could travel about 20 miles per hour—four times the speed of Fulton's river steamboat, the *Clermont*.

McKay and the *Flying Cloud* More than 500 clipper ships were built between 1845 and 1860. Many of those that were built in the United States came from Donald McKay's shipyard in Massachusetts. McKay, who was born in Nova Scotia, Canada, had established a shipyard in East Boston in 1848.

In this engraving, the artist shows shipbuilding as it was in McKay's time.

Most of McKay's clippers were about 200 feet long and capable of carrying about 1,500 tons of cargo. One of McKay's most famous clippers was the *Flying Cloud*. This sleek and beautiful boat was launched in 1851. At 235 feet, it was the largest clipper in the world at the time of its launch. His largest clipper, launched in 1853, was named the *Great Republic*. It measured 335 feet in length and was able to carry about 4,500 tons of cargo.

Clipper Trips After the discovery of gold in California in 1848 and then in Australia in 1851, trade across the Pacific increased. Migration from the eastern part of the United States to California also increased. When the news of California gold reached the East, thousands of people rushed westward in the hopes of striking it rich.

The *Flying Cloud* was launched shortly after the discovery of gold in northern California, and much of its fame was linked to this event. Following its launch, the *Flying Cloud* made the trip from New York City to San Francisco, California, in a record 89 days. The famous clipper ship repeated this record-making journey in 1854.

Around Cape Horn Ships traveling from the Atlantic westward to the Pacific had to travel the full length of the South American continent and around its southern tip at Cape Horn. Despite the advent of steamboats in the 19th century, the trip around South America favored sailing vessels. Few refueling stations existed at the time along the South American coast, and most steampowered vessels could not carry enough coal or wood on board for such a long journey.

Launched three years after the discovery of gold in 1848 in California, the *Flying Cloud* broke all records for the journey from New York to San Francisco, completing the trip in 89 days.

Decline of the Clippers

Clipper ships became popular at the same time that steam-powered vessels were starting to cross the ocean in increasing numbers. Although clippers relied on sail power and were faster than most large steam-driven ships, one of their main drawbacks was their size. The trade-off for size was speed—the smaller the ship, the faster it could travel.

But as trade increased, merchants wanted to ship more goods. Many clipper ships began to transport Australian wool. But speed was not important for the wool trade. By the late 1800s, larger, square-rigged sailing vessels and ships powered by steam engines were taking over the business that the clippers had enjoyed in the 1840s and 1850s.

Another blow to the clippers traveling the Atlantic route was the opening of the Suez Canal in Egypt in 1869. Before the Suez Canal, clippers traveled around the tip of southern Africa while plying the tea trade between India, Europe, and the United States. The Suez Canal cut thousands of miles off the journey from the Atlantic to the Indian Ocean. Speed in the open seas no longer mattered in the way it had before.

In the 20th century, ships underwent great changes in design and use. As passenger travel faced increasing competition from airlines, ships became larger and more luxurious. Cruise ships now have air conditioned cabins and swimming pools. Cargo ships now are designed and classified by the type of cargo they carry. For example, tankers transport liquid cargo. Container ships carry packed goods, such as electronic products or furniture, in large aluminum boxes that resemble railroad freight cars. Since most of the globe is covered by water, it is likely that ships will always be around.

The Otis Elevator

The invention of the elevator revolutionized architecture and led to the construction of skyscrapers.

Getting Off the Ground

The elevator may seem like an unusual invention to include among transportation milestones. Most of the dramatic innovations in transportation have involved moving people quickly from one place to another. The elevator fits that category perfectly. Tall structures, such as the Egyptian pyramids and buildings of more than one story, have existed since ancient times. The usual mode of transportation from lower to higher levels was by foot.

Like people today, the inhabitants of the ancient world did not particularly enjoy breathless and exhausting climbs to high places. Like their 20th-century counterparts, they looked for ways to make life easier.

In about 230 B.C., the Greek mathematician Archimedes actually invented a type of elevator. It was operated by ropes and pulleys and human or animal power. But elevators did not become practical until a source of inanimate power—the steam engine—was discovered.

Steam Safety The steam engine contributed to the development of elevators as it had with many other modes of transportation. By the mid-1800s, elevators run by steam engines had begun to appear in the United States. The engine provided the power that pulled the cables up and down, thus raising and lowering the elevator to different levels. But these early elevators were used almost exclusively to haul freight from one level to another.

People feared elevators—and with good reason. When the cables broke, as often happened, the elevator had only one place to go: down! And the greater the distance it had to fall, the more likely that passengers would be seriously injured or killed. Therefore, people preferred to walk up and down stairs. The few elevators in existence were used mainly in warehouses, coal mines, and other kinds of businesses.

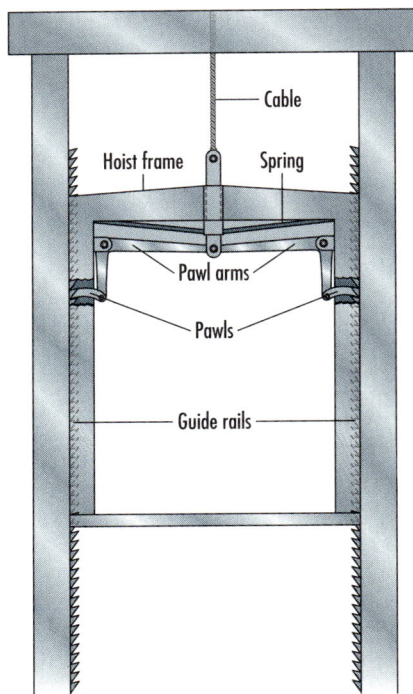

Cable
Hoist frame
Spring
Pawl arms
Pawls
Guide rails

The addition of a special spring and pawl device made elevators safe.

By making elevators safe for passengers, Elisha Otis enabled architects and builders to design and construct taller buildings.

The Safety Hoist

The person who made elevators safe for people was Elisha G. Otis of Yonkers, New York. Otis was certain that if elevators could be made safe, they would have a great future and a profound effect on life in the United States. Otis set about designing a safety device that would prevent an elevator from falling if its cables broke. In Otis's safety hoist, or safety elevator, the pulling cable was attached to a special spring at the top of the hoist. The pull of the cable bent the spring and retracted a pawl, a single "tooth" on each side of the frame. This kept the pawls from engaging the notched guide rails on which the elevator ran. If the cables broke, the spring straightened and forced the pawls to engage the guide rails. This then stopped the elevator from falling.

In 1853, Otis successfully demonstrated the new safety device on a freight elevator on which he himself was riding. The success of the demonstration inspired confidence in elevators for passengers. In 1857, the first elevator designed exclusively for the

In 1893, the Otis Elevator Company demonstrated its new and improved elevator at the World's Columbian Exposition.

use of passengers was installed in a store in New York City.

Otis profited handsomely from his invention. In 1861, he founded a company to manufacture elevators and secured a patent on a steam-powered elevator.

New Sources of Power Steam-powered elevators had several drawbacks. They were noisy and did not have a reliable source of power. Engines had frequent breakdowns and a continual need for repairs. The fledgling elevator industry needed a new source of power.

Hydraulics In 1846, English inventor William Armstrong successfully demonstrated a hydraulic crane. Hydraulic machines use the pressure in a liquid—water or oil—to move a piston (a sliding rod) within a cylinder. Force applied to the cylinder raises the pressure throughout the system. This, in turn, causes the desired action to occur.

It soon became apparent that elevators and hydraulics were made for each other. Hydraulically powered elevators sit atop a huge metal piston inside a liquid-filled column sunk into the ground. Pressure produced in the system forces liquid into the column, making the elevator rise.

Reducing the amount of liquid in the column makes the elevator descend.

The first hydraulic elevators began to appear in the 1870s and quickly replaced the steam-driven ones. But hydraulic elevators required a column sunk into the earth as deep as the building was tall. So there were practical limits to the height they could reach.

Electricity In 1889, the first electrically powered elevator was installed. Electricity was clean, efficient, and soon the most available source of power. Elevators no longer needed coal, oil, or water in order to work.

Today, some builders of skyscrapers are putting their elevators on the outside of the building, giving passengers a spectacular view of the surrounding area.

A Common Sight

Early electric elevators needed special operators. The starting device was usually a large metal handle that was pushed from side to side to start and stop the elevator. Elevator operators were trained in how to line up the elevator with the floor—something that today is a part of the automatic mechanism of self-service elevators. In addition to raising and lowering the elevator, the operator opened and closed the heavy metal gate that enclosed the elevator car. The operator also opened and closed the door on each floor. Such early elevator designs are still in evidence today. Warehouses and loft buildings still have large freight elevators that need trained operators to run them. But regular elevators—such as the ones in apartment and office buildings and large multistory stores—are "automatic," or self-operated.

The first automatic elevators were small, private compartments installed in the homes of very wealthy people. There were many such elevators in New York City in the 1890s. Large automatic elevators began appearing in office buildings in the 1950s. Today, some elevators have a computer-generated voice calling out floor numbers as the elevator reaches them.

Elevators had an enormous influence on modern architecture. Skyscrapers would have been unthinkable without electric elevators. Modern electric elevators can move at speeds of more than 1,800 feet per minute. This is especially important when moving tens of thousands of people to and from their offices, as is the case in New York City's World Trade Center or Chicago's John Hancock Center, at the start and close of each business day.

23

The London Underground

The city of London built the world's first subway system and revolutionized travel within large cities.

A Choked City

In the mid-1800s, London, England, was not a pretty place. The capital city of Great Britain and the British Empire was the richest city in the world—and also one of the most congested.

By 1850, London's population had swelled to 2.7 million people. A quarter of a million people came into the city each day to work in the bustling factories and businesses. Horse-drawn buses and cabs, private carriages, vendors selling from pushcarts, and people on foot all competed noisily for room to move about the city. London was choking on traffic and filth. Its narrow streets, some of which dated back to Roman times, turned into rivers of mud during rainy weather. The great and historic center of British culture was suffering from massive gridlock.

One solution according to some planners was to bring railroads from the surrounding areas farther into the city. At the time, London was served by numerous privately run railroad lines. But rivalry between rail companies, as well as the objection of many Londoners, prevented the extension of these railroads into the city.

The idea that was finally approved was to build a new railway within the city itself. This line would run beneath the streets while in the city and would connect with the rail lines just outside the city that went to other parts of England. A special corporation—the Metropolitan Railway Company—was formed to plan and build it. With the approval of Parliament and the city government, work began on the first small stretch of what was to become the greatest subway system in the world: the London Underground.

This drawing from 1860 shows the work in progress on the King's Cross underground station in central London.

The Hole in the Street

Digging up the streets of London to build an underground railroad was no small job. The streets were not only clogged with people, horses, and traffic. They were also the site of many homes and businesses. The people who lived and worked in them would have their lives disrupted for years while construction went on.

People who lived at that time have described what it was like to have their streets dug up. First, traffic was cleared, creating an unaccustomed sense of quiet. But suddenly, the calm was shattered by the arrival of steam engines, carpenters, delivery wagons hauling loads of wooden planks, and armies of workers with shovels and pickaxes.

The inconvenience was great. The amounts of soil brought to the surface as the tunnel was dug created mountains of dirt, much of which found its way into homes and businesses. Buildings adjacent to the construction site were often propped up with timber to prevent them from sliding into the construction area.

This kind of project in the middle of a major city had never been undertaken before. Accidents were bound to happen. More than once, a cave-in left timber and machinery tossed together at the bottom of the tunnel. But in the end, the job was done.

The London "Tube"

The Metropolitan Railway's line opened officially in 1863, carrying passengers from Farrington Street, on the edge of the old city of London, to the district of Paddington, four miles away.

These first trains of the London Underground were powered by steam engines. The tunnels were sufficiently ventilated to allow smoke to escape, but there were problems. Soot tended to accumulate on the tracks, sometimes making traction difficult.

In 1890, the first electrified rail line was opened. Electrical power was provided by a special "third rail"—a separate rail parallel to the two tracks. A mechanism on the train connected the cars to the third rail. This additional rail fed electricity to the train's engine and thus provided power.

Gradually, all the lines were converted to electricity. By 1905, the system was totally electrified.

The "tube," as the Underground is unofficially called, became a bomb shelter during World War II. At the height of the German bombing of London (1940–1941), hundreds of thousands of Londoners used the Underground as an air raid shelter. On one evening alone in September 1940, more than 175,000 people slept in stairwells and on station platforms while German bombers rained death and destruction on the city above.

The Underground Today Since its opening in 1863, the London Underground has continued to grow.

During World War II, Londoners sought shelter from German bombing raids in the Underground. Here children sleep in hammocks slung between the rails.

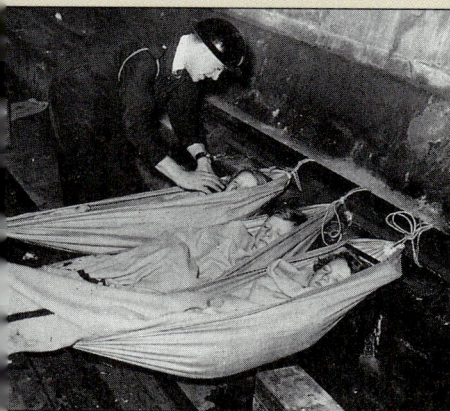

SUBWAY SYSTEMS AROUND THE WORLD

City	Year Opened	Current Length of Route (in miles)
London, England	1863	255
Boston, Mass.	1897	30
Paris, France	1900	171
Berlin, Germany	1902	67
New York, N.Y.	1904	232
Buenos Aires, Argentina	1913	40
Tokyo, Japan	1927	102
Moscow, Russia	1935	114
Montreal, Quebec	1966	22
Beijing, China	1969	14
Washington, D.C.	1976	22
Hong Kong	1979	10

Nearly a century later in 1962, the government approved a new line, the first since 1907. Today, the London Underground has about 275 stations and 11 separate lines servicing all parts of London and its suburbs. Although the Underground is considered a single system, it was built over the decades by several different private firms. As a result, its construction varies from line to line. Some lines are very deep below ground, while others actually have stretches that operate on the surface, especially on the outskirts of the city.

The London Underground connects with British Railways at London's major long-distance railroad stations—Paddington, Victoria, Euston, Waterloo, and Charing Cross. London's Underground does not stay open all night. Most lines stop running shortly after midnight and resume service around 5 A.M. Some stations are closed on weekends. Fares on the Underground are based on the distance traveled. The London subway carries millions of riders each day, not only within the city but to and from the outlying areas as well.

Here is a list of subways in some of the world's major cities.

Subways of the World

Following London's lead, subways became a major part of the transportation systems of many large cities around the world. In Europe, major subways were built in Paris (1900), Berlin (1902), Madrid (1919), and Moscow (1935). Although none of these lines are anywhere near as large as London's, each is distinctive. Moscow's subway stations, for example, are noted for their elaborate construction, statues, mosaics, and fine chandeliers.

Boston constructed the first subway line in the United States, which began operating in 1897. New York City's system, which rivals London's in size, opened its first line in 1904. The Washington, D.C., rapid transit system was begun in the 1970s. Although each of these subway systems is unique, they share a common function. They move millions of people quickly and inexpensively from place to place while relieving traffic in the streets.

The Pullman Car

The invention of the folding upper berth improved the railway sleeping car and made long-distance travel easier.

The first Pullman cars featured seats that converted to beds and beds that folded out of sight when not in use.

Long Night's Journey

Imagine the thrill of an overnight railroad journey in the United States during the 1850s. America's growing rail system took travelers in record time to places they had never seen before. Rail passengers journeyed over mountains and across rivers into states that had previously been difficult to reach by horse and wagon—or even by canal barge or riverboat.

George Pullman's training as a cabinetmaker was helpful in designing sleeping compartments.

Exciting, yes; but imagine also the exhaustion and aching back of the traveler when he or she arrived at the destination. The reason was that travelers had to sit up in their seats all night long. Early railroad cars had very crude sleeping accommodations or, most likely, none at all. In addition, seats were often made of hard wood and were not upholstered. Even if the train was not crowded, stretching out for hours on a hard wooden bench provided little comfort.

As more and more people traveled across the United States on the growing rail network, the need for comfortable sleeping arrangements on overnight trips became very important. A New York inventor and businessman named George Pullman met that need.

A New Age in Rail Travel

Foldaway Beds George Mortimer Pullman was born in Brocton, New York, in 1831. His early professional training was as a cabinetmaker. But Pullman's real interest was in railroad cars. In the mid-1850s, while still in his early twenties, George Pullman began experimenting with a design for railway sleeping cars.

In 1858, having moved to Chicago, Pullman was hired by the Chicago & Alton Railroad to convert two old railway cars into sleeping cars. But Pullman was interested in more than simply redoing old coaches. Over the next few years, he designed an entirely new sleeping car, which he called the *Pioneer*. The innovation that made the name so appropriate was startlingly simple: foldaway beds. Thus, a simple seat by day converted into a comfortable bed at night. An upper berth, or sleeping compartment, which was tucked out of sight during the day, could be pulled down to make a bed at night.

This was the earliest "Pullman car." In 1865, it was introduced into service on the Chicago & Alton line, marking a new age in rail travel. That same year, the *Pioneer* carried the slain body of President Abraham Lincoln from Washington, D.C., to Springfield, Illinois.

A Clever Businessman George Pullman not only had a mind for invention, he was also a clever businessman. He realized that railroad travel could be improved in a number of ways—and that he could make millions in the process.

In 1867, he formed his own manufacturing company. The Pullman Palace Car Company, as he called his new firm, made only one product—Pullman cars. In 1868, Pullman added another feature to his railroad cars—one that would have a far-reaching effect on rail travel. He created the first dining car, which was fully equipped with its own kitchen.

Before the introduction of dining cars, long-distance travelers had to bring along their own food for the journey. The dining car changed all that. A special car fitted out with dining tables and chairs, menus and waiters, enabled travelers to enjoy a freshly prepared meal and the passing scenery.

Dining on a moving train had its drawbacks, of course. The meals were expensive and were therefore limited to those who could afford them. Less well-to-do travelers still had to provide their own food. On these early trains, which were greatly affected by the twists and turns in the tracks, a bowl of delicious hot soup might end up in the diner's lap or on the floor. Nevertheless, the addition of dining cars and sleeping cars vastly increased the comfort level of long-distance travel and brought much new business to the railroad industry.

Although modern sleeping cars are more comfortable than the originals, the principle remains the same—convertible seats and foldaway beds.

Pullman's Name Is Tarnished By the 1890s, George Pullman's company had a sleeping car monopoly. Not only did he make the cars, he also owned them and employed the porters who worked on them.

As his business empire grew, Pullman built his own company town near the manufacturing plant on the outskirts of Chicago. He expected his workers to live there. This arrangement made workers completely dependent on Pullman's goodwill. They not only worked for him but lived in his housing and bought food in his stores. This eventually created an unhappy situation.

George Pullman's name is attached to a dark episode in American labor history. In 1894, when labor leaders attempted to persuade Pullman's workers to join the union, a worker's strike was brutally crushed by Pullman and the federal government. Hundreds of workers were seriously injured, and Pullman became known for his poor treatment of workers and suppression of unions.

An Important Legacy
Although Pullman may not be remembered as an enlightened and caring businessman, he left an important legacy to the nation's transportation history.

Sleeping cars are still known as Pullman cars, even though their design and manufacture have undergone enormous changes since Pullman's time. Although many different kinds of sleeping cars are in operation today, the basic feature of the convertible berth is still used in most of them. One of the most recent cars, the Amtrak double-decker, has sleeping accommodations on its upper level and freight-carrying space on its lower level. Dining cars are a regular part of most trains traveling over long distances.

Pullman's genius was not only in his inventive ability. It was also in his early recognition that railroad travel would be a significant part of America's growth as a nation. With that understanding, he set about making rail travel as comfortable and as enjoyable as possible. In so doing, he helped the railroad industry prosper and become a major part of the U.S. economy.

The *Spirit* of St. Louis

Charles Lindbergh made the first nonstop solo flight across the Atlantic and stimulated interest in air travel.

The New York Times.

LINDBERGH DOES IT! TO PARIS IN 33½ HOURS; FLIES 1,000 MILES THROUGH SNOW AND SLEET; CHEERING FRENCH CARRY HIM OFF FIELD

The world virtually held its breath until the newspapers announced the success of Lindbergh's solo flight across the Atlantic Ocean.

A Man for the Times

The 1920s was a period of "firsts." People were fascinated with setting records—whether it was sitting for days atop a flagpole or dancing in a marathon until they dropped. As airplanes became more sophisticated in design, fliers also sought to set—and break—records.

One of the most formidable challenges facing any aviator of the time was the Atlantic Ocean. During the early 1920s, some fliers had tried to fly nonstop across the Atlantic from America to Europe. But they were never heard from again.

In the mid-1920s, a talented and ambitious young American aviator named Charles Lindbergh decided to give it a try. Lindbergh was born in Detroit in 1902. He developed an early interest in aviation that led him to quit college and join the army. There he trained as a pilot. In 1925, when his service in the army was completed, Lindbergh took a job flying mail in the Midwest. It was a time of small planes and daring stunts. Aviators, no matter where they flew, needed courage—and luck.

"The Lone Eagle"

Lindbergh had the courage to try the transatlantic flight, but he also was shrewd enough not to leave too much to luck. In order to succeed in his venture, Lindbergh guessed that he would have to design and build a plane specially equipped to make such an unprecedented flight.

Building a plane, however, required money. To underwrite the cost of the project, Lindbergh approached a group of nine businessmen in St. Louis, Missouri. Eager for the windfall of publicity that would come if the flight succeeded, the businessmen funded the project.

In honor of his benefactors, Lindbergh named the plane the *Spirit of St. Louis*. It was built in San Diego, California. A single-engine aircraft, the *Spirit of St. Louis* was designed to carry extra fuel—much more than would normally be stored on a plane

of this size. The plane, which is on display in the National Air and Space Museum in Washington, D.C., is so small that most people would probably not want to take a joy ride in it—much less fly across an ocean.

Destination: Paris! In 1927, Lindbergh flew the *Spirit of St. Louis* from San Diego to Long Island, New York, on May 10—making only one overnight stop.

Weather and technical problems delayed the main flight for another ten days. Finally, on May 20, 1927, Lindbergh took off from Roosevelt Field on Long Island and headed out over the Atlantic. His destination was Paris, France. For the next day, the world held its breath. Air-to-ground radio communications were primitive, and Lindbergh was out of touch for most of the flight. He had taken sandwiches on board for his meal, but for most of the flight, he fought against cold and exhaustion.

Thirty-three and a half hours after leaving the United States, he made it. Lindbergh touched down at Le Bourget Airport outside Paris.

The world went berserk. Overnight, Charles Lindbergh became everybody's hero. The shy young flier was mobbed by reporters and adoring crowds. He was given ticker tape parades and was awarded the Congressional Medal of Honor by President Calvin Coolidge. Lindbergh's face appeared in newspapers and on magazine covers the world over. In a celebrity-obsessed decade, Lindbergh was the idol of his day.

A Tarnished Idol Charles Lindbergh lost much of his glory when he decided to speak out on foreign policy issues. In the late 1930s, he supported America's isolation from the growing crisis in Europe. He admired the brutal, anti-Semitic Nazi regime of Adolf Hitler in Germany.

Throughout 1940 and 1941, as Europe fell to the Nazis, Lindbergh opposed American intervention. When the United States declared war on Japan and Germany in December 1941, Lindbergh became a discredited figure. Although he wanted to fight for his country and applied for a commission in the Army Air Corps, President Franklin Roosevelt turned him down.

TRANSOCEANIC TRAVEL (NEW YORK TO PARIS)		
	Time	**Capacity**
Spirit of St. Louis	33½ hours	1
Boeing 747	7 hours	345
Concorde	3½ hours	100
Queen Elizabeth II	5 days*	1,700

*New York to Southampton, England

Several modern methods of transatlantic travel are compared to Lindbergh's famous flight.

The Real Contribution

The *Spirit of St. Louis* inspired many copycat attempts to cross the Atlantic Ocean, and more people died. One who succeeded—American Amelia Earhart—became the first woman to fly nonstop across the Atlantic. But she did so in the company of two men.

Although he remained an aviator, Lindbergh's 1927 flight was the pinnacle of his flying career. The fame it earned him made him a constant object of public curiosity, especially after his young son was kidnapped and murdered in 1932.

Lindbergh spent much of his life promoting American civil aviation. In his later years, he became a strong supporter of environmental causes. He understood the importance of aviation and used his fame to support the growth of commercial air travel. As a consultant to the airline industry, he lived to see the day of commercial jet aviation. In many ways, his contribution to the growth of aviation overshadows the momentary dazzle of his flight across the Atlantic Ocean. Lindbergh died at his home in Hawaii in 1974.

The *Spirit of St. Louis* is now part of the permanent exhibit at the National Air and Space Museum in Washington, D.C. This view gives an idea of how small the plane actually is.

The Autobahn

Built in Germany during the 1930s, the world's first superhighway enabled vehicles to travel faster over longer distances.

Nazi leader Adolf Hitler breaks ground for the Autobahn, the superhighway system that was supposed to provide jobs and bring Germany out of its economic troubles.

The Car and the Road

Roads have existed in civilization for thousands of years. The Romans built a vast network of roads—the most famous of which was the Appian Way—to connect their far-flung empire. In the United States, the first major hard-surfaced road was built in Pennsylvania in 1794. But most travel in early America was done on waterways or on small roads near towns and cities.

High-speed highways developed as a result of the spread of the automobile in Europe and America. By the 1920s, more and more people were buying automobiles. Most countries had to build new road systems to accommodate the increasing numbers of vehicles.

The world's first modern highway was built in Germany in the 1930s. As a nation, Germany had been united only since 1871. Prior to unification, it was a collection of dozens of princely states, duchies, and other political entities. It had no system of national roads connecting one part of the country to another. And it needed one.

Hitler's Highway

The road system that is the pride of Germany today was begun during that nation's darkest period. The first German superhighway, called the Autobahn, was the brainchild of Nazi leader Adolf Hitler.

Hitler came to power in 1933 and intended to make Germany the most powerful nation in Europe and the world—by whatever means. He supported any idea that showed Germany as a nation of power and influence. A system of highways would obviously bring prestige to the Germans, especially when compared to the inadequate road systems of neighboring European countries.

Symbols and Realities The Nazis regarded the Autobahn as a symbol of Germany's power. On a more humble level, a road system would connect all parts of Germany and help to further unify the country.

In conjunction with the development of the road system, the Nazis also built a new kind of automobile—a "people's car," or Volkswagen, as it has come to be known around the world. The Volkswagen was intended to be an inexpensive car that the average German could afford. The idea was that millions of people would buy them and, of course, drive them on an Autobahn.

The original intention never became a reality under Hitler—Volkswagens did not become available to the people. Engineers built a prototype, and mass production was scheduled to begin in 1941. But World War II altered the plan. The Volkswagen had to wait until after the war before it became a success.

The Autobahn system, however, was built. The first stretches of the network connected Germany's largest cities, such as Munich, Dresden, Leipzig, Berlin, Hamburg, and

Artillery and supplies for the Allied (Britain, Soviet Union, and United States) war effort speed along the Autobahn.

Frankfurt. The Autobahn was originally constructed as a four-lane highway, with two lanes in each direction and the inner lanes reserved for fast driving.

A Road to Nowhere Hitler and his officials made a great commotion every time a portion of the Autobahn system was either begun or finished. The Nazis held grand ceremonies commemorating the latest success. Hitler—with shovel in hand and striking the pose of a worker—presided over these events.

But the Autobahn network remained relatively underused during the 1930s and 1940s. The "people's car" had not materialized, and vast stretches of road had only a few vehicles on them.

Ironically, the Autobahn network proved to be a quick and efficient route for U.S. and Soviet tanks when they invaded Germany at the end of World War II. The excellent German engineering held up well to the heavy treads of thousands of tanks as they rumbled across the devastated country.

After the war, the German government continued to build the Autobahn network. By the late 1980s, more than 5,100 miles of road had been constructed, with connecting roads to smaller German towns and cities. The original stretches of the Autobahn have been expanded to six-lane modern superhighways. They look no different from any modern highway in the United States.

Superhighway Issues

Today, the German highway system is connected to the major highway systems of other countries in Europe. Like most superhighway systems, the Autobahn is heavily traveled. The German system, however, has earned a notorious reputation as a dangerous road system populated with fast and reckless drivers. The Autobahn network has no official speed limit. Drivers often top 80 or 90 miles per hour—significantly faster than the speed limit on U.S. interstates.

The growth of superhighways around the world has raised issues other than speed and safety. A superhighway displaces a lot of people and nature when it is built. Millions of cars and trucks traveling on these superhighways emit pollutants into the environment.

Many of these issues still need to be addressed. Despite these ongoing problems, it is difficult to imagine a modern industrial nation without superhighways.

Today, the Autobahn is comparable to superhighways everywhere, such as this one near Harrisburg, Pennsylvania.

The Helicopter

Because it can fly straight up and down, the helicopter has many special uses.

An Old Idea Revived

The use of helicopters—all kinds of helicopters in many different ways—is a relatively recent development. But the idea of a machine that could fly straight up and down has been around for hundreds of years.

In the late 1400s, Italian painter and inventor Leonardo da Vinci designed a device that was supposed to be able to fly straight up into the air. In the late 1700s, several French inventors made drawings and even scale models of machines that resembled helicopters. None of these flying machines was actually built.

Engines for Flight These early "inventors" lacked one major element to make their fantasies come true: a source of energy to propel their machines. In 1876, German engineer Nikolaus Otto invented and patented an internal combustion engine and changed all that. Otto's engine produced power by burning fuel within the engine.

In 1903, when Orville and Wilbur Wright showed that a human-made device with an engine attached could fly and stay aloft, all kinds of aviation became possible. The Wright brothers' first runway was a stretch of beach in North Carolina. The airplanes that eventually evolved from their original design required a great deal of space to accelerate and gather enough speed to lift them off the ground.

While early aviation focused on airplanes, some engineers set out to build a different kind of flying machine. Reviving an old idea, this machine was designed to overcome the force of gravity and rise straight up in the air without the need for a long runway. The successful invention came to be called the "helicopter."

Off the Ground

Early Visionaries The first flight by a human being in a helicopter prototype occurred in France. In 1907, an inventor named Louis Bréguet built a machine with four rotors. While his assistants held tightly to it—just in case it threatened to fly out of control—Bréguet's flying machine rose two feet off the ground and stayed in the air for one minute.

Later that same year, a French engineer named Paul Cornu stayed aloft for about 20 seconds and reached a height of about six feet. This was the first free flight, one not held to the ground during the flight.

Over the next 30 years, many inventors continued to experiment with helicopterlike machines. Whatever their approach, they all seemed to be interested in reaching the same goal—to keep improving the machine so that it could fly higher and for longer periods of time.

Igor Sikorsky, sitting unprotected in the open air, is shown here piloting his first helicopter.

A Better Helicopter A major breakthrough in the quest for a better helicopter occurred in 1937, when a craft designed by German engineer Heinrich Focke flew to a height of 8,000 feet over a distance of 76 miles. Focke demonstrated that helicopters—despite their peculiar appearance—had moved from being elaborate toys to being seriously considered as an important mode of transportation.

In the United States, Russian-born inventor Igor Sikorsky built and piloted the first practical single-rotor helicopter in 1939. During World War II, the U.S. and British governments explored the military uses of Sikorsky-type helicopters. Although helicopters did not play any significant role during that war, they soon developed into a major weapon.

How Does It Work? A helicopter works by seeming to defy gravity. A helicopter's lift is provided by a set of horizontal blades—called rotors—above the body of the helicopter. The rapidly whirling blades create air currents beneath them that literally lift the helicopter straight into the air.

However, in order to prevent the helicopter from turning in circles in the same direction as the blades, other rotors and a tail are needed. On some helicopters, smaller rotors on the tail stabilize the helicopter and prevent it from turning out of control in the direction of its main rotors.

Helicopters move forward when the pilot tilts the main rotors in the direction in which he or she wishes to fly. Reducing the rotor speed lowers the helicopter back to the ground. The rapidly whirling blades create a "chop-chop-putt-putt" sound, which is probably the origin of the helicopter's nickname of "chopper."

The Black Hawk helicopter is equipped with powerful engines that enable it to lift more than 8,000 lbs. of military equipment.

An Explosion of Uses

The early inventors and designers of airplanes probably had little idea how important aviation would become in the 20th century. Similarly, the designers of the helicopter could not have predicted the many different ways in which it would be used.

The helicopter came into its own during the 1950s. Large transport helicopters were used during the Korean War (1950–1953) to carry troops and equipment to and from the fighting front.

But U.S. participation in the Vietnam War in the 1960s and the early 1970s saw the final evolution of the helicopter into a war machine. During that conflict, guns, cannons, and even jet engines were added to fast-flying, lightweight helicopters. These "helicopter gunships" were easy to maneuver and could locate and fire on enemy positions in remote places.

Peacetime Uses Outside the military, people have found many different ways to use helicopters. One of these uses is in rescue missions—at sea, on mountains, in rivers—in any place where the helicopter's maneuverability is crucial. Aerial observation has become another important way to use choppers. Radio and TV stations regularly use helicopters for traffic reports in and around cities. Police departments use helicopters with high-powered beams of light to keep track of police activities on the ground. In agriculture, helicopters have been used to seed and dust crops.

The development of heavyweight helicopters capable of hauling cargoes has led to a variety of industrial uses. One industry that depends on these heavier machines is offshore oil drilling. Helicopters transport workers and heavy equipment between land and the offshore drilling site.

This odd little invention that people had dreamed about for so many centuries has turned out to be an important part of the modern transportation network. In situations that call for speed and maneuverability, the helicopter can usually perform the task.

The Jayhawk, shown here, is designed to fly long distances on a tank of fuel.

Kon-Tiki

A Norwegian anthropologist showed that Polynesians may have originally come from South America.

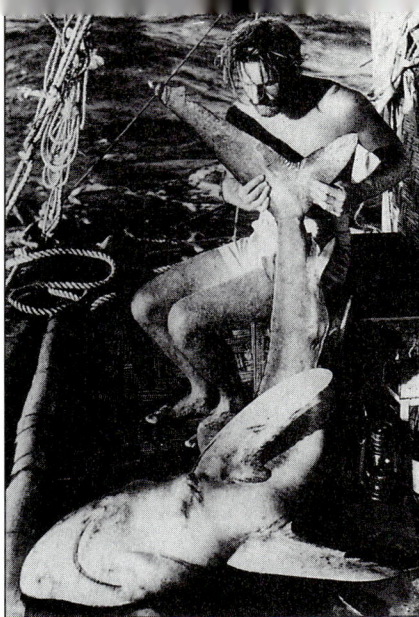

In 1947, Norwegian anthropologist Thor Heyerdahl set out to prove his theory that Polynesia was settled by people who came from South America.

Early Travels

Anthropologists study the cultures of the different peoples of the world. Until relatively recently, however, they had little understanding of how these people made long trips across great oceans thousands of years ago. If such voyages indeed occurred, they would have been made in very small and flimsy boats.

In the 1930s, the Norwegian anthropologist Thor Heyerdahl studied cultures in the South Pacific islands and in North and South America. In the course of his studies, he discovered certain similarities between the early Native Americans of western South America and the Polynesian peoples of the South Pacific.

Heyerdahl found, for example, that Polynesians and South American Indians had certain physical and cultural similarities. They did not use metal of any kind, but both had weaving, pottery, and the wheel. Equally important, many elements of their folklore and myths were strikingly similar.

Polynesia and South America are separated by more than 4,000 miles of the Pacific Ocean. Most anthropologists believed that the Polynesians came originally from Asia, which is to the west. But was it possible, Heyerdahl wondered, for early Polynesians to actually have come from the east—from South America? Despite the huge expanse of ocean between the two regions, could early South Americans have sailed westward on small rafts and settled in what is now Polynesia?

The raft Kon-Tiki was constructed from the same materials that Heyerdahl believed the travelers used about 1,500 years ago.

A Daring Experiment

Heyerdahl decided to test his theory by making such a trip on a small raft. His success would prove that early peoples could also have crossed the Pacific.

Building the Raft Thor Heyerdahl's first task was to build a raft similar to those he believed were used by the ancient inhabitants of South America. Early in 1947, he assembled a crew of five and set off for the South American nation of Ecuador. Deep in the jungles there, the crew chopped down balsa trees and peeled off the bark, in the same manner as the native peoples before them. They tied nine large logs together with hemp, because the earlier peoples would not have used nails or metal of any kind to secure the logs.

Then the crew floated the raft down rivers to Peru. In the harbor at Callao, the crew added two masts with a small sail between them and an open cabin made of bamboo. Its roof was made of banana leaves. For safety's sake, the crew took a few "modern" conveniences—lanterns and a radio transmitter to keep in contact with observers on land. Heyerdahl and the crew named the raft

Kon-Tiki for the legendary Peruvian who supposedly led his people across the Pacific to Polynesia about 1,500 years before.

Six Men and a Bird On the morning of April 28, 1947, the *Kon-Tiki* was towed out of the harbor at Callao to begin its long journey. Thor Heyerdahl, his five crew members, and a green Peruvian parrot were on board. The parrot was a good-luck companion for the voyage.

For several weeks, the *Kon-Tiki* drifted in a cold current off the coast of South America. Once the raft sailed clear of this current, the water became warmer. The warm waters provided the crew with a wide variety of fish for their diet. In fact, sometimes there were too many fish. During stormy weather, high waves tossed fish onto the raft. And at night, all sorts of fish became stranded on the deck. The crew gathered them in the morning, put the edible ones aside for dinner, and threw the others back into the water.

Not all their neighbors were so friendly. Schools of sharks often followed the raft. In order to get rid of them, the crew lifted them by hand onto the deck, where they died. Although some varieties of shark are edible—and even tasty—these were much too salty and were thrown back into the sea.

Lonely Days at Sea Heyerdahl and his companions had no idea how long they would be at sea. They were not even sure that their mission would be successful. Days dragged into weeks. Everyone on board shared the chores, such as cooking and making repairs to the raft. The crew took turns piloting the *Kon-Tiki* in two-hour shifts. For recreation, they read, took photographs, sang songs, and

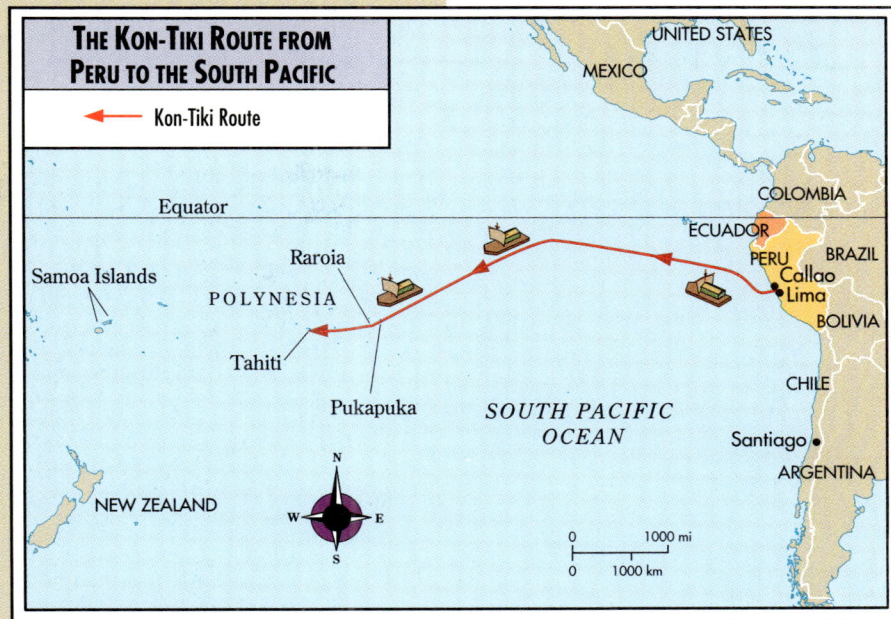

THE KON-TIKI ROUTE FROM PERU TO THE SOUTH PACIFIC

← Kon-Tiki Route

The 4,000-mile journey made Heyerdahl and his five-member crew instant celebrities.

played with the parrot. Sometimes they simply stared with wonder at the vastness of the ocean.

Land! After 93 days at sea, the crew sighted land. A few days before, they had noticed birds flying over the raft. The crew tried to steer in the direction of the birds' flight. They hoped that would lead them to land.

Then, on July 30, the Polynesian island of Pukapuka loomed in the distance. But currents and winds pulled the raft back to sea. Eight days later, on August 7, the *Kon-Tiki* approached Raroia, an uninhabited island surrounded by a coral reef. Suddenly, wind and waves pushed the raft onto the knifelike coral, where it became trapped. As the *Kon-Tiki* pounded against the reef, the crew abandoned ship in order to save their radio and other possessions.

The *Kon-Tiki* was severely damaged on the reef and was towed to Tahiti. The journey had come to an unexpected but successful conclusion.

A Theory Proved

Thor Heyerdahl's daring experiment made him an instant celebrity. More important, however, was the fact that it proved that such a journey could have been made by early Peruvian Indians, despite the small size of their craft and the many dangers of such a long voyage.

Heyerdahl soon began to wonder if early inhabitants in other parts of the world had made similar journeys. In 1970, he tried to make the same kind of trip across the Atlantic Ocean. This time, he tested the possibility that early Mediterranean peoples had sailed to the West Indies. In the *Ra-2,* a replica of an ancient Egyptian boat made from papyrus reeds, Heyerdahl crossed the Atlantic. He sailed from the northern African country of Morocco to Barbados in the West Indies.

Some anthropologists still dispute Heyerdahl's claims. Even so, he has given them reason to consider that ancient peoples may indeed have made long and dangerous journeys across vast oceans centuries before European explorers.

Vostok I

The voyage of *Vostok I* in 1961 marked the beginning of human space travel.

What's Out There?

Human beings have wondered about outer space for thousands of years. Even today, a generation after the first humans traveled into space, many people still wonder about UFOs and the possibility of life on other planets.

Scientists had long suspected that space travel could answer many questions about how the sun, the planets, and the stars were formed. Space travel might even determine whether life exists beyond the earth's atmosphere.

The invention of the airplane in the early 20th century proved that humans could resist the earth's gravity enough to fly. Space travel, however, required far more sophisticated equipment and a greater scientific understanding.

The Challenges For human beings to journey into space, a number of challenges had to be overcome.

- Life had to be protected in the oxygen-free environment that exists above the earth's atmosphere. Therefore, an enclosed environment with adequate oxygen was necessary for humans to breathe.

- That enclosed environment had to be strong enough to resist the enormous physical pressures of leaving and reentering the earth's atmosphere. A weak and insufficient vehicle would burn to ashes from the fiery power of reentering the earth's atmosphere.

- The vehicle traveling into space would need enormous power to escape gravity and the earth's atmosphere. Such power could never come from an airplane engine, no matter how strong it was made. Special rocket engines would have to be developed.

- Once in space, humans would need the ability to communicate with people on the ground. Space communication and navigation depended on advances in computer and radio technology.

- Finally, takeoff and landing sites would be needed.

Meeting the Challenges

Funding, before anything else, was needed to make it possible to meet these challenges. Without the commitment of massive amounts of money over a long period of time, no space program could be developed.

In the United States, plans for a venture into space began in 1945 after the end of World War II. Several presidents and the Congress realized that government would have to bear the brunt of the costs if a space program was to succeed. But the U.S. government did not make space travel a priority until America's arch-enemy in the 1950s—the Soviet Union—became the first nation to place spacecraft into orbit.

The Shock of *Sputnik* A stunned and bewildered America woke up on the morning of October 5, 1957, to discover that, one day earlier, the Soviet Union had launched and put into orbit a grapefruit-sized satellite, named *Sputnik*. A crisis of confidence immediately gripped the American public.

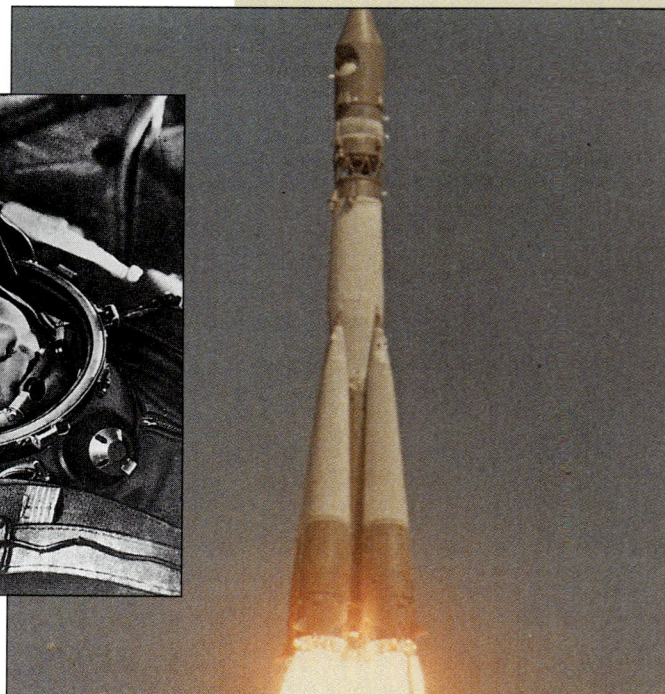

The Soviet Union and cosmonaut Yuri Gagarin stunned the world in 1961 when a man successfully went into space. Gagarin is shown here in his space capsule (inset) next to the launch of his spaceship *Vostok I.*

Where had America gone wrong? How could a repressive and dictatorial system beat American ingenuity and democracy in the space race?

There were no easy answers, but *Sputnik* was a "wake-up call." The U.S. government and private industry focused their efforts on putting an American into space.

Another Soviet Success On April 12, 1961, the Russians did it again. A spacecraft named *Vostok I* blasted off from a remote area in the Soviet republic of Kazakhstan. It carried on board the first man to travel in outer space. His name was Yuri A. Gagarin, and he and *Vostok* made one full orbit of the earth.

Gagarin had met the basic challenges of space flight. He had proved that a human being could escape the earth's atmosphere and return safely. While in space, he had communicated with people on the earth as clearly as if he had been in an ordinary airplane.

Ten months later, the United States followed the Soviets with its first manned orbital flight. John Glenn, later a U.S. senator from Ohio, circled the earth three times on February 20, 1962, before landing safely in the waters off the coast of Florida.

From the beginning, space travel was caught up in the rivalry between the Soviet Union and the United States. In many respects, the rivalry was probably healthy, in that it stimulated efforts toward further research and development in the field of space exploration.

The success of the *Vostok I* flight led to greater achievements in space. Throughout the 1960s, orbital flights became longer. In addition, a greater number of scientific experiments were undertaken on these flights.

U.S. space research turned to the development of a reusable spacecraft—the space shuttle. One is shown here landing at the Kennedy Space Center at Cape Canaveral. Following the landing, a drag parachute is opened to slow down the spacecraft.

The Present and the Future

At first, the Soviet Union maintained an edge over the United States. The Soviets tried several group flights in which two cosmonauts, in separate spacecrafts, orbited the earth simultaneously.

In 1963, Soviet cosmonaut Valentina Tereshkova, the first woman in space, orbited the earth 49 times. In the mid-1960s, crews of three and more people went up. In 1965, an American astronaut came out of the space capsule and "walked" (actually floated) in outer space. He was protected by a space suit equipped with oxygen.

Great Achievements In 1969, the United States landed the first men on the moon—an achievement that made up for the early humiliation of *Sputnik* and *Vostok*. The Soviets turned their expertise toward the building of space stations. This program culminated in the 1986 launch of *Mir*, a station where astronauts could spend weeks or months conducting experiments.

In the 1970s, American research and development turned to the development of a reusable space shuttle. The shuttle was intended to carry astronauts into space for research and to deliver and retrieve other space satellites.

The U.S. space shuttle program suffered a catastrophic setback on January 28, 1986, when the shuttle *Challenger* exploded shortly after taking off from Cape Canaveral, Florida. All seven astronauts on board were killed. Several years later, shuttle flights resumed, again with a focus on scientific research.

A Cloudy Future The future of space travel in both the United States and Russia remains unclear. The U.S. Congress and the public in the 1990s seem less interested or dazzled by space exploits. As a result, the level of government funding has declined in recent years. The Russian effort has been seriously altered by the collapse of the Soviet Union in 1991 and the resulting political and economic chaos. Most experts find it difficult to predict where space exploration will go now, three decades after the success of *Vostok I*.

The TGV

❦

France's high-speed train opened a new era in railroad travel.

The fastest and smoothest train in the world, France's TGV runs at an average speed of about 170 mph. The early versions of the TGV covered the 267-mile trip from Paris to Lyons in two hours. Newer models can run at 250 mph.

A Century of Innovation

During the 20th century, transportation made remarkable leaps in aviation and automobile travel. At this time, railroad designers were also seeking ways to improve rail travel and to keep it an important part of modern transportation.

Railroad travel had always been a major—and popular—means of travel in Europe. The automobile came to Europe at the same time it did to the United States. But Americans adopted it with more enthusiasm and more quickly than Europeans. One reason was that Europe had been devastated by two world wars between 1914 and 1945. Countries were destroyed and populations were very poor. For Europeans, an automobile was a luxury that few could afford. Another reason for the lack of popularity was that distances in Europe were not as great as in America. European rail travel was relatively inexpensive and efficient. Therefore, it remained the major means of transportation.

The Aftermath of War After the turmoil of World War II, much rebuilding was necessary. Roads and rail lines throughout Europe had been demolished by bombs. The supply of railroad cars and engines had been severely reduced by the fighting.

In the late 1940s, the United States established the Marshall Plan, a program to provide massive aid to help the countries of Europe rebuild. European governments were called upon to establish their priorities for reconstruction.

The Revival of Railroads The governments of Europe—especially those of France and Germany—moved quickly to rebuild their railroads. They spent large amounts of money to do so. The situation was very different in the United States. In Europe, the means of transportation were owned and operated by the government. In the United States, however, transportation was a private matter—owned and operated by private corporations. Whatever government money was spent on transportation construction went mainly into the building of roads, especially the U.S. interstate highway system. Rail transportation became more of a freight operation and less concerned with moving passengers. By the late 1950s, airplanes and the automobile were replacing railroads as the preferred means of travel among Americans.

French Rail Advances

In many respects, advances in modern railroad design became the province of the French. Their most significant contribution to rail travel was the development of the TGV—*train à grande vitesse*—the train of great speed, which began operating in 1981.

Designed to be the fastest train in the world, the TGV was intended for quick travel between cities. For that reason, it was also called the "intercity train."

How Good Is It? The TGV travels at an average speed of over 165 miles per hour, twice as fast as an ordinary train. The speed advantage attracted potential motorists. If they could save time by train, why bother driving?

In addition to speed, the TGV posed a double threat to the airlines—cost and convenience. Although tickets on the TGV train are more expensive than on regular trains, they are still cheaper than airline tickets. Furthermore, the TGV offers a special convenience for travelers. Most railroad stations are in or near the center of town, and most airports are

HIGH-SPEED TRAINS			
Country	**City**	**Train**	**Average Speed**
France	Paris	TGV	165 mph
Japan	Tokyo	Shinkansen ("Bullet Train")	160 mph
England	London	British Railways Intercity 125	125 mph
United States	New York/ Washington, D.C.	Amtrak Metroliner	80 mph
Canada	Toronto/ Montreal	The "Rapido"	80 mph

Several countries have high-speed rail lines. But only Japan's "bullet train" comes close to approaching the speed of the TGV.

miles—sometimes many miles—from the cities they serve. Because intercity trains went from one downtown railroad station to another, the TGV eliminated the time and need for transportation between the airport and the city.

What's It Like on the TGV? For Americans, many of whom have never ridden on a long-distance train, the TGV is an eye-opening experience.

To begin with, there is the thrill of its astonishing speed. No train currently in use in the United States can match the lightning speed of a TGV ride. A 267-mile trip from Paris to Lyons is finished in about two hours. A trip of roughly the same length in the United States—between New York City and Washington, D.C., for example—takes four hours on a conventional Amtrak train and three hours on Amtrak's fastest train, the Metroliner.

Another surprise on the TGV is the service. American commuters, who are familiar with staggering through lurching cars looking for a snack bar, are amazed to be served dinner in their seats on the TGV.

These trains are also equipped with barbers, beauty salons, gift shops, fax machines, and telephones. For the bustling business traveler, the TGV leaves little to be desired.

TGVs do not operate only in France. One can travel throughout most of western Europe on the TGV. Overnight trips are no problem because the TGV provides comfortable sleeping compartments.

Japan's fully electric streamlined trains complete the 350-mile trip between Tokyo and Osaka in 3 hours and 10 minutes.

Several countries are experimenting with trains without wheels. Called *maglev* (for magnetic levitation), these trains are operated by a system of giant magnets and electricity.

Other Nations Follow

Other industrial nations have also developed high-speed trains. Japan's Shinkansen "bullet trains"—named for their bulletlike speed—move travelers quickly and comfortably between Japan's major cities.

Even the United States seems to have finally realized the advantage of high-speed rail travel. Amtrak is currently experimenting with high-speed locomotives.

At a time when airline fares are rising, and when the public is more conscious of the harmful effects of auto pollution, state and federal governments are trying to improve passenger rail travel. In 1993, for example, New York State announced a plan to build a high-speed magnetic train—one capable of traveling more than 200 miles an hour between New York City, Albany, and Boston. Unlike the TGV, which runs on conventional rails, a magnetic train runs along a single rail guideway and is controlled by magnetic fields.

The Concorde

Flying faster than
the speed of sound,
the Concorde dramatically
reduced the flight time
between Europe and
the United States.

Faster Than Sound

The speed of sound is about 760 miles per hour. To fly faster than that became possible only after the invention of rocket-powered and jet-powered aircraft. Until the 1940s, airplanes were powered by propeller-driven engines. The fastest of these airplanes flew no more than 300 miles per hour.

With jet engines, planes could begin to approach the speed of sound. To actually break the sound barrier, engineers had to solve two problems. They needed still more powerful engines. And they needed sturdier planes. Existing designs could not survive the shock waves that hit the planes at high speeds, causing them to break apart.

Once a plane did break the sound barrier, another problem had to be considered—noise. When a plane flies faster than sound, the air it cuts through expands rapidly behind it. This expansion creates a sonic boom—a frighteningly loud noise that is heard on the ground.

Moving Toward SST

The first successful steps in the development of a supersonic transport (SST)—a plane that flies faster than the speed of sound—were made by the U.S. military. In 1947, the Bell Corporation built an experimental aircraft called the Bell X-1. Piloted by the now-famous aviator Chuck Yeager, it became the first aircraft to fly faster than the speed of sound. The Bell X-1, however, was powered by rockets, not jet engines.

In 1953, the North American F-100 Super Sabre became the first jet fighter that operated at supersonic speeds. Five years later, the first commercial jet aircraft went into service. In 1970, a Pan American World Airways Boeing 707 began regular passenger service between New York City and Paris.

The Boeing 707 and the other commercial jets that followed it into passenger service flew between 550 and 600 miles per hour at their fastest speeds. These speeds were still well below supersonic levels.

A Joint Effort

Airplane designers did not rest with the development of jet passenger planes. In Europe, the French and British governments made a joint decision to cooperate on the design of an SST, to be called the Concorde. The aircraft industries and the governments of those countries realized the enormous cost of designing and producing such a plane. They agreed to share the costs—between both countries and between government and private industry.

The United States aircraft industry was not as fortunate. After first helping to support the Boeing Company in the design and manufacture of an SST, the U.S. Congress voted to end funding for the project in 1971. The reason given was the high cost of the project. Thus ended hopes for an American SST.

The Concorde Flies—Maybe

In 1969, the Concorde made its first test flight. Whatever engineering problems it faced were simple to solve compared to the difficulties it faced on its road to passenger service.

In order to be successful economically, the Concorde had to fly to the United States. But many environmentalists were opposed to granting landing rights to the SST. They feared that the exceptionally loud noise the plane made when it broke the sound barrier would damage the environment, disturbing both humans and wildlife.

In 1947, aviator Chuck Yeager broke the sound barrier. His plane, the Bell X-1, is on permanent display at the National Air and Space Museum in Washington, D.C.

For those who can afford the ticket price—about $7,000 for a round-trip ticket from New York to London—the Concorde is the quickest and most luxurious way to travel.

A Luxury Flight The Concorde is very expensive to fly—about four times the cost of regular transatlantic flights. The narrow plane holds only 100 passengers, but they enjoy a flight of total luxury. A Concorde passenger is not aware when the plane breaks the sound barrier and reaches its cruising speed of 1,350 miles per hour. The only difference from ordinary flights that passengers are aware of is that at the enormous heights at which the Concorde flies, they can actually see the curve of the earth.

In the United States, the Concorde continues to fly to New York and Washington. But only the wealthy and those on expense accounts can afford to fly it. As a popular means of travel, the SST has achieved only limited success.

A Limited Success

After years of negotiation and compromise, the Concorde was finally allowed to land in the United States—on a very limited basis. In 1976, Concorde flights began between Washington's Dulles International Airport and London (on British Airways) and Paris (on Air France). The following year, the Concorde was allowed to land at John F. Kennedy International Airport in New York.

In order to avoid disturbing those who live and work near the airport, the Concorde was prohibited from flying at supersonic speeds until well out over the ocean. Even with this restriction, the Concorde made the trip in record time compared with a conventional jet.

Flying the Concorde A British Airways Concorde leaves London every day at 10:30 in the morning and arrives in New York at 9:20 the same morning—50 minutes "before" it took off from London. This strange bit of time travel is caused by the fact that London time is five hours ahead of New York time and the flight across the Atlantic Ocean is less than

five hours. The total time taken to fly from London to New York is 3 hours and 50 minutes—three hours faster than the same trip on a Boeing 747. When the Concorde arrives in New York, it is afternoon in London but still morning in New York.

Over the years, the development of more powerful engines has enabled airplanes to go faster.

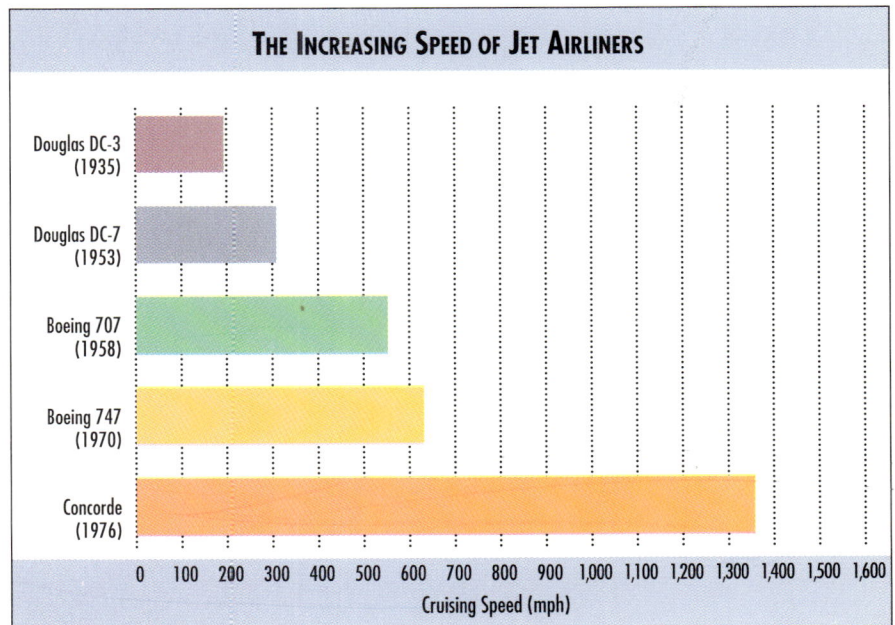

THE INCREASING SPEED OF JET AIRLINERS

Aircraft	Cruising Speed (mph)
Douglas DC-3 (1935)	~200
Douglas DC-7 (1953)	~300
Boeing 707 (1958)	~550
Boeing 747 (1970)	~625
Concorde (1976)	~1,350

Cruising Speed (mph)

The Gossamer Condor

In 1977, a lightweight human-powered aircraft flew two miles and won a prize.

Throughout history, human beings have been fascinated by flight. This early flying machine was designed in 1807 by Jacob Degen. It is not known whether he ever built it.

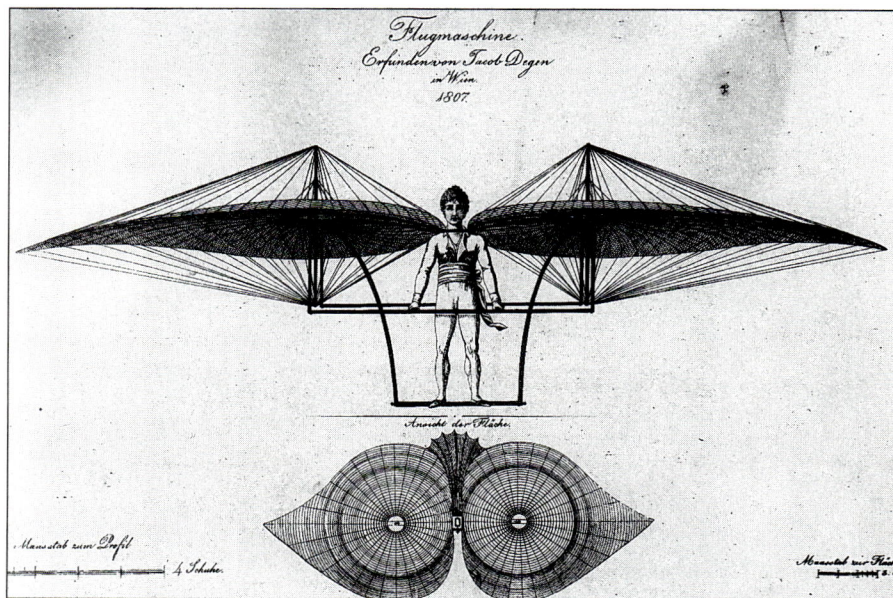

To Fly Like a Bird

When humans first thought of flying, they naturally looked at birds to see what could be learned from them. The wings of birds seemed to flap up and down. (In fact, they move in a semicircular motion, and this type of movement is what allows birds to fly.)

But human beings who lived centuries ago did not fully understand the principles of aerodynamics, or motion in air. Their first attempts at flying were usually made with flapping wings attached to their arms in what they thought was an imitation of bird flight. The results were always disastrous.

The great Italian painter and inventor Leonardo da Vinci sketched a machine with birdlike wings in the 1480s. Leonardo's machine was never built, but his drawing marks the beginning of the scientific study of flight.

With centuries of frustration behind them, people interested in flying turned their attention away from imitating bird flight. They began to concentrate on inventing machines that could fly.

Machine Power Wins Out

In 1783, the age of human flight began when the Montgolfier brothers of France lifted off in their balloon. Balloons turned out to be only one branch of flight. When Orville and Wilbur Wright first flew their airplane in North Carolina in 1903, modern aviation began.

Balloons and aircraft, no matter how different, do have one thing in common: neither is propelled by human power. Balloons are lifted by lighter-than-air gases or by the expansion of heated air. Although airplanes have wings, they do not rise because their wings flap. Airplanes rise because powerful engines move them with enough speed to enable the wings to produce lift.

An Unending Fascination The fascination with human-powered flight persisted well into the 20th century. In 1959, British industrialist Henry Kremer announced a prize of £50,000 (about $150,000) for anyone who could fly a human-powered aircraft over a particular course. That course was two miles long and was shaped like a figure "8."

Trying for the Kremer prize required both engineering know-how and personal daring. The challenger would have to do more than strap on a set of wings and jump off a cliff with arms flapping. He or she would need a thorough understanding of the principles of flight and a strong knowledge of aviation design.

A Team Assembles From 1959 until the 1970s, no one had been able to win the prize. Then Paul B. Mac-Cready assembled a team of American engineers and produced a machine called the *Gossamer Condor.* The goal of the design team was to create an aircraft using the right

Bryan Allen, the man who flew the *Condor,* trained on this custom-made bicycle to build his strength and endurance. During the actual flight, he generated nearly one-half horsepower—about four times the power of a recreational cyclist.

What's Ahead?

Human-powered aircraft like the *Gossamer Condor* and the *Gossamer Albatross* were made possible by the availability of strong, lightweight materials and by a thorough understanding of aerodynamics. But what practical use do human-powered aircraft have? The answer is, probably very little. It is difficult to imagine a world in which the skies are full of people in their personal *Gossamer Condor*s as they pedal to and from school or work. Nor does there seem to be a future use as freight-bearing aircraft.

The *Gossamer Condor* seems more important as a symbol of humankind's ability to overcome obstacles and a continuing desire to accomplish the impossible. Just as the modern jumbo jet is testimony to the continuing evolution of scientific knowledge, so is the *Gossamer Condor* an example of human expertise and ingenuity. The *Gossamer Condor* was donated to the Smithsonian Institution in Washington, D.C., where it has become a permanent part of the exhibit at the National Air and Space Museum.

combination of lightweight materials that would enable a person to maneuver it. On the other hand, they wanted to construct a machine that would be durable enough to withstand the wind pressure and not be blown apart.

Obviously, most of the materials used to make conventional aircraft could not be used on the *Gossamer Condor*—with one exception: aluminum. This light metal is used to make the outer skin of modern airplanes. The wings and fuselage of the *Gossamer Condor* were covered in polyethylene film, the material of dry cleaning bags. In 1977, the *Gossamer Condor*—consisting of aluminum, cardboard, and plastic parts held together with piano wire—was unveiled as a competitor for the Kremer prize.

Once strapped in, the pilot pedaled until the craft achieved sufficient speed to rise into the air.

The first flight was a success, and the *Gossamer Condor* won the prize. The pilot was Bryan Allen, a California biologist and competition bicyclist. In 1979, Allen pedaled another lightweight aircraft across the English Channel—a significantly longer flight than the two-mile course for the Kremer competition. The craft used in this exploit was called the *Gossamer Albatross.* In 1987, an American named Glenn Tremml pedaled a craft called the *Eagle* through the air for 37 miles. The next year, Greek cyclist Kanellos Kanellopoulos flew the *Daedalus* 74 miles over the Mediterranean Sea.

Californian Paul MacCready designed and built the *Gossamer Condor.* He won the Kremer prize when Bryan Allen completed a figure "8" course while remaining 18 feet off the ground.

How It Worked The *Gossamer Condor* was a product of careful engineering and sophisticated knowledge of aerodynamic principles. It worked, however, in a relatively simple way. The pilot used his or her feet to pedal the machine into the air— like an airborne bicycle.

The pilot's seat was placed below and at the center of the *Gossamer Condor*'s 29-foot-long single wing.

Glossary

aerial: Related to or occurring in the air.

aerodynamics: The study of the motion of air and other gases and forces acting on bodies moving in air.

anthropology: The study of the cultures of different peoples of the world.

archaeology: The study of the way humans lived a long time ago as shown by fossils, artifacts, tools, and ruins they left behind.

astronomy: The study of the sun, the moon, planets, stars, and other heavenly bodies.

aviation: The design, production, and operation of aircraft.

balsa wood: A lightweight but strong wood especially useful for building rafts and boats.

bamboo: A tall, woody grass with strong, hollow stems that can be used for building.

barge: A flat-bottomed boat used to carry freight on canals or rivers.

barrage balloon: A balloon, tied to the ground, that is used as protection against air attacks. It is sometimes employed to support nets that are used as obstacles against low-flying enemy aircraft.

blimp: A nonrigid, buoyant airship filled with a gas, usually helium.

Bronze Age: The period in human history from about 3500 B.C. to 1000 B.C., characterized by the use of bronze tools and weapons.

bullet train: Japan's Shinkansen train, so named because of its speed and sleek design. The term may also be used to describe any high-speed train.

catacomb: An underground passageway with small rooms for tombs. In the early days of Christianity, catacombs were used as worship and burial places.

chopper: A nickname given to a helicopter, probably because of the sound made by its rapidly moving blades.

circumnavigate: To go completely around something, especially by water.

clipper ship: A fast sailing ship, especially one with a tall mast, large sails, and an overhanging bow.

coral reef: A hard, stony deposit that forms near the surface of the ocean and consists of the skeletons of millions of tiny sea animals. Coral reefs may be very colorful and run in chains many miles long.

dirigible: A giant, cigar-shaped balloon with a rigid metal interior frame attached to a passenger cabin and engines.

environmentalist: A person concerned with the quality of the earth's environment, especially the conservation of natural resources and the control of pollution.

folklore: The customs, beliefs, and stories of a certain group of people that are handed down from one generation to another.

gear: A toothed wheel that interlocks with another in order to transmit motion.

gridlock: A traffic jam in which the grid of intersecting streets is so congested that there is little or no traffic movement.

horse train (packtrain): A caravan of horses and travelers who band together for long trips, such as the journeys westward during colonial times.

hull: The sides and the bottom of a ship or a boat.

hydraulics: The branch of science that deals with the behavior of liquids under pressure or in motion.

magnetic train: A train that runs along a single rail controlled by a magnetic field.

Marshall Plan: A program of the late 1940s in which massive aid was provided to help Europe rebuild after World War II.

mass production: The making of goods in large quantities, especially by machinery.

meteorology: The study of the earth's atmosphere and the changes that occur within it, including the study of weather.

monopoly: The sole ownership or control of a product or service by one person or company.

mortar: Building material made of sand, lime, and water, which is used like cement to hold bricks or stones together.

nomadic: Having to do with nomads, people who wander from place to place in search of food and pasturelands.

paddle wheeler: A steamboat propelled by a paddle wheel—a large wheel with paddles fixed around its circumference.

Polynesia: One of three groups of South Pacific islands east of Australia and the Philippines.

prairie schooner: A covered wagon used by pioneers to travel across country; a variation of the Conestoga wagon.

prototype: The first example of something, upon which later models are based or judged; also, the first full-scale model of a new type of vehicle, machine, or other device.

rotor: One of a set of horizontal blades on a helicopter, which create air currents that cause the helicopter to lift straight up into the air.

smelt: To melt ore in order to separate the metals from it.

sonic boom: A shock wave produced by an aircraft when it exceeds the speed of sound. It is often audible on the ground.

sound barrier: A sudden and large increase in resistance exerted by the air on an aircraft nearing the speed of sound.

Sputnik: The first artificial satellite launched into space by the Soviet Union on October 4, 1957; also, the name of a series of Russian satellites that followed this first one.

steamboat: A boat powered by steam, especially a shallow vessel used on inland waterways.

Stone Age: The period in human history from about 2 million years ago to about 3000 B.C., characterized by the use of crude stone tools.

supersonic: Faster than the speed of sound.

supersonic transport (SST): An aircraft that flies faster than the speed of sound.

Tour de France: A famous annual bicycling event in France. The world's best bicyclists compete in a race of more than 2,500 miles.

transatlantic: Extending across the Atlantic Ocean.

Suggested Readings

Note: An asterisk (*) denotes a Young Adult title.

Ballantine, Richard, and Grant, Richard. *Richards' Ultimate Bicycle Book*. Dorling Kindersley, 1992.

*Boyne, Walter J. *Smithsonian Book of Flight for Young People*. Atheneum, 1988.

*Davies, Eryl. *Transport: On Land, Road, and Rail*. Franklin Watts, 1992.

Fisher, Leonard E. *Tracks Across America: The Story of the American Railroad*. Holiday House, 1992.

*Graham, Ian. *How Things Work: Cars, Bikes, Trains, and Other Land Machines*. Kingfisher, 1993.

*———. *Space Science*. Raintree Steck-Vaughn, 1992.

*———. *Transportation*. Raintree Steck-Vaughn, 1992.

Grosser, Morton. *Gossamer Odyssey: The Triumph of Human-Powered Flight*. Houghton Mifflin, 1981.

Hawkes, Nigel. *Structures: The Way Things Are Built*. Macmillan, 1993.

*———. *Vehicles*. Macmillan, 1991.

Heyerdahl, Thor. *Kon-Tiki*. Simon & Schuster, 1991.

*Jefferis, David. *Flight: Fliers and Flying Machines*. Franklin Watts, 1991.

*Kentley, Eric. *Boat*. Knopf, 1992.

*Lafferty, Peter, and Jefferis, David. *Pedal Power: The History of Bicycles*. Franklin Watts, 1990.

Lindbergh, Charles A. *We*. Buccaneer Books, 1991.

*Macauley, David. *Underground*. Houghton Mifflin, 1976.

———. *The Way Things Work*. Houghton Mifflin, 1988.

**Rand McNally Children's Atlas of World History*. Rand McNally, 1991.

*Randolph, Blythe. *Charles Lindbergh*. Franklin Watts, 1990.

Siegel, Beatrice. *The Steam Engine*. Walker & Company, 1986.

*Spangenburg, Ray, and Moser, Diane K. *Living and Working in Space*. Facts on File, 1989.

*———. *Opening the Space Frontier*. Facts on File, 1989.

Taylor, Michael. *History of Flight*. Outlet Book Company, 1991.

Time-Life Books. *Transportation*. Time-Life, 1993.

**The Visual Dictionary of Flight*. Dorling Kindersley, 1992.

**The Visual Dictionary of Ships and Sailing*. Dorling Kindersley, 1991.

*Williams, Brian. *Pioneers of Flight*. Raintree Steck-Vaughn, 1990.

*Williams, Owen. *How Roads Are Made*. Facts on File, 1989.

Index